BITTER-SWEET
RECOLLECTIONS

Sermons on the
Old Testament Lessons
Lent and Easter Seasons
Series A

Barbara Brokhoff

0238/ISBN 0-89536-638-X   PRINTED IN U.S.A.

Lovingly dedicated to "MY JOHN,"
Teacher without peer
(in my opinion),
World's greatest preacher,
second only to Dr. James Stewart (also my opinion),
Husband, lover, and friend without equal
And the man I STILL can't beat at tennis!

CONTENTS

1
Kindness That Makes You Sorry!

Ash Wednesday
Joel 2:12-19

".... Now return to the Lord your God, For He is gracious and compassionate, slow to anger, abounding in lovingkindness, and relenting of evil." (NAS)

A gentle Christian of the Society of Friends, a lady by the name of May Haviland, lived alone. One night as she entered her bedroom, she found a burglar rifling through her bureau drawers. When she turned on the light, he pointed a gun at her heart. She gently said to him: "Put that thing away. If there's one thing I can't stand, it's guns. Besides, if your need is so great you have to steal, then you must need my things more than I do." She not only gave him what he was pilfering, but shoved money into his hand, all the while expressing concern for the circumstances he must be facing. The next day she found all her possessions in her box, along with a note which read, "Lady, I can face anger and danger and death itself, but I was powerless before your kindness!"

The kindness of God is the basis for answering the call to return and repent in today's first lesson. Ash Wednesday is a time for us to check ourselves on our faith. Just as at the beginning of the new year we take inventory and make new resolutions, so Ash Wednesday begins for us the Lenten period of taking stock of our direction and perhaps adjusting to a new heading. Our orientation point is Good Friday's cross. That is the landmark which identifies whether we are off-course or not. From the heading of that tree-cross, we make corrections for our lives. We are called, in this text, to "return," to repent, to turn around. Far too often the days of our lives are spent in the frantic pursuit of what pleases the "self." Today's emphasis, in our world, is on number one — what pleases "me." Lent will be a time of heart-break (rending our hearts, not our garments), as we learn to die to self. Before we can rejoice in Easter's resurrection, we must mourn and weep over our sins. It is a time of repenting and returning to God. It is a journey with Jesus to suffering and death.

Most of us, when we are really being honest with ourselves, know we need to confess our sins — not just in general, but specifically. What sins? Sometimes we are malicious, unkind, jealous, proud, irritable, intolerant, judgmental, impure. We pull off slick business deals. We tell the "expedient" lie. We hurt the name or reputation of another with spiteful gossip. We lose our tempers. In a hundred ways, we do what we know is wrong and fail to do what the inner voice of the Spirit prompts us as right. We try to convince the world that we are wiser, better, younger, smarter (or whatever) than we really are. We are so adept at deception that we have even managed to fool ourselves. But in doing all of these things, God's peace has been blocked out of our lives, and we are empty. Lent calls us back to reality and repentance.

The discipline and self-denial of repentance is never easy, but if we expect to rise with Christ in newness of life on Easter, we must walk the Calvary road of death to self, to sin, to rebellion, and to stubborness.

Joel's call is clear: "Return" — but what is there to make us "want" to repent? A small child was playing on a cold day, wading barefoot in a deep puddle of water. His father, a believer in "permissive parenthood," stood nearby. A friend stopped and said, "You'd better get that boy out of that cold water before he catches pneumonia." The father replied, bewilderedly, "I know, I know, I'm trying to think of something that will make him want to!"

God is no bumbling, confused, permissive parent who doesn't know how to handle his wayward, sinning children, but his very nature is motivation for our repentance.

God Is Slow to Anger

Some folks get mad at the slightest thing. They are volatile, explosive, and easily angered. Nearly two million crimes are committed in the U.S. each year because of anger. Anger leads to a half-million divorces a year or more. More than 100,000 people are killed in accidents of some kind because of loss of emotional control. Almost any small disagreement is cause for boiling fury. I saw a cartoon which showed a husband and wife having breakfast in a fine, large home. Obviously they had been arguing. They looked angry, sullen, and bitter. She was shouting at him, "O.K., O.K.! You want a hot breakfast? Then set fire to your cornflakes!"

Disagreements between persons are so frequent we almost think nothing of them. Murdo McDonald, a fine Scot preacher, tells of a time when Lady Astor became very angry one day at Sir Winston Churchill and hissed at him across the room: "If I were your wife, I would put poison in your food!" Churchill stood up, bowed gallantly, and said, "Madam, if I were your husband, I would gladly take it!"

Every day we see fireworks in the home, at school, on the job, on the tennis court, on the golf course, on the highways — short fuses — that's what most of us have, but not God! The Old Testament is filled with accounts of his long-suffering in spite of the fact that he is rejected, disobeyed, and ignored. He bore with the ugly ways of the murmuring nation of Israel as he led them out of bondage in Egypt toward the Promised Land. He gave them chance after chance, until his anger could no longer be contained. Saul, the first king of Israel, displeased God, disobeyed him often, but in great patience and slowness of anger, God gave him one opportunity after another to repent and change his ways. Surely most of us can remember the long-suffering of God who has shown his reluctance to anger as he has dealt with our repeated sins and wrong-doings.

It must be thoroughly understood that a gracious and merciful God, even though he *is* slow to anger, nevertheless *can* be angered. Slow to anger he is, but the Divine wrath is never to be trifled with but rather to be feared. Let us never presume upon the mercy of a compassionate God who is slow to give us the punishment we rightly deserve!

God Is Kind

Joel says that God is "abounding in loving-kindness." The *King James Version* says, he is "of great kindness." It is true that we all deserve to die for our sins, there is no doubt about it. But even when we are unlovable, God loves us anyway. He always has enough love, mercy, and grace to forgive us!

Think of the thoughtless, unkind, heated words you spoke in sudden anger to someone lately. The words hurt, injured, and maybe even destroyed that person. Can the injured party forgive you, or want to?

Maybe so, maybe not, but God can!

Think of a teen-age girl who runs away from home, lives with one man after another without benefit of marriage, becomes addicted to drugs, finally becomes pregnant, and after breaking her parents' hearts by ignoring them, decides to go home to have her baby, allowing her parents to take care of her. Can the parents forgive that? Can they love her anyway? Some parents can, some can't, but God can!

Think of the unfaithful husband who, after an adulterous relationship, comes home and gives his wife Herpes which he has contracted; then he asks forgiveness for his promiscuity. Can she forgive? Some can, some can't, but God can!

The "great kindness" of God is completely beyond our understanding. We can only bask in the marvelous realization that it is so. Recently, the son of atheist Madylan Murray O'Hair wrote that without faith, things don't seem to work. He tells how his mother buys a Cadillac every year, yet she doesn't have it a full year until it falls apart. She lacks faith in everything. She gets a phone, and it won't work. She can buy a dozen roses on Monday, and they are dead on Tuesday. He says, "It's a part of the vibrations, and over-all, they are negative vibrations. It destroys everything around her. I've never seen anything like it!"

You'd think that, in view of our sinfulness, we'd get bad vibes and quiver with fear before a holy God whom we have wronged. Rather, we get only good vibrations from God, for he is so very compassionate and kind. Frederick W. Faber wrote a lovely hymn, one stanza of which says:

"For the love of God is broader,
Than the measure of man's mind,
And the heart of the Eternal

Is *most wonderfully kind.*"

The Apostle Paul found the same to be true, for he said, in Romans, " . . . the kindness of God leads you to repentance."

God Relents of Evil

God relents when we repent! The gracious, lovingkindness of God is more ready to relent than we are to repent. He stands anxiously waiting to jump at the chance to restore us to fellowship in the Divine Presence, that relationship that was destroyed by our sinning.

God despises all sin, but even though his justice must still mete out judgment and punishment, he constantly looks for ways to become less severe with us. God, unlike us, does not hold a grudge.

For many years, there was a sign in front of a man's yard in a small town in north Georgia. It stood atop a huge pile of dark, ugly aluminum sheets. It was a large, sandwich type sign, lighted at night, and could be read from some distance away. Other than the ugly sign and dirty metal, the house was painted a sharp white, the grass was kept mowed, flowers bloomed in profusion, but all the neatness and beauty was marred by the sign which cluttered the whole place. Apparently, the owner of the house had had a bad experience with the aluminum and decided to "get even" with the company. The sign read: "This Alcoa Aluminum with 30-year guarantee is no good!" So, holding to his grudge, year after year he ruined his own landscape in order to declare his displeasure.

God is much more gracious than that. He does not seek revenge upon us. Joseph Stalin once said, "To choose one's victim, to prepare one's plans minutely, to stake an implacable vengeance, and then to go to bed — there is nothing sweeter in the world."

If we got what we deserved, we'd all be in hell. Revenge and retaliation may be what *we* seek when we are injured, but not God. The story is making the rounds of the rich Texas rancher who threw a big party for all his friends. In order to have some special fun, he filled his huge pool with man-eating sharks. Then, at a given time, he invited the guests to stand around the pool while he announced that anyone who would jump in and swim across the pool would be given one of three things : "You may have my ranch, a million dollars, or the hand of my beautiful daughter in marriage." Just then a commotion at the other end of the pool made everyone look that way. One man had jumped in and was frantically swimming for the other side, desperately fighting off the sharks in the churning water. By some miracle, he made it safely to the other side, and the rancher was dumbfounded. "I didn't think *anybody* would take me up on that offer," he said, "but I'm a man of my word, so the deal goes. What do you want: my ranch, a million dollars, or my daughter?" The man shouted, "I don't want any of those things!" The shocked Texan said, "All right, you name it and you've got it." The man said, "I want the guy who shoved me into that pool!"

God's justice calls out for punishment, but more than anything else, he wants to be gentle, not harsh, with us. His longing is to see us repent, so that he can relent of the evil which we have brought upon ourselves.

Kindness That Makes You Sorry

I came to know Christ as my Savior after hearing many, many sermons and refusing far too many invitations to be a Christian. I'd heard preaching about the Great Judgment Day, sermons about hell-fire and brimstone, messages that vividly described hell as a place of wailing and weeping and gnashing of teeth, and sermons that sometimes nearly scared me to death. Several times, I almost decided to confess Christ, not because I really felt any urgency for repentance, not because I was sorry for my sins, but because I was "caught."

Then one day I heard a preacher tell the story of Calvary's cross in love. He described the great lovingkindness of the Son of God, hanging there, dying for *me*. Near the end of the sermon, he said, "Close your eyes, forget the minister, forget who's sitting next to you, forget the past, forget everyone and everything else, and think. Then realize that if you were the only sinner in the world, he would still have done it, just for you. Then listen — and pray — and, by faith, look in your mind, up to that cross. Then listen again, and Christ will speak to you: 'I did it for you, Barbara, because of your sins. I died that you might live!'" Young as I was, I decided to do it, and seeing him there, in agony and blood, my heart and my stubborn will were broken. For the first time in my life, I *wanted* to know Christ, not to escape hell, but to *know* him. No longer did it matter if my friends or family understood, no longer did it matter that everyone in the church already thought I was a Christian, no longer did I love my sins — but now, seeing him, loving him, and sorry for my sins, I made my way to the altar, gave my life to him and was baptized. It was ultimately his kindness that won me and made me sorry!

2

The Blessing Of Bondage

First Sunday in Lent
Genesis 2:7-9, 15-17; 3:1-7, 21

The Bible's story of Creation and the Fall gives rise to all sorts of stories, like this one: Adam and Eve were walking near the Garden of Eden, showing it to their son, Abel. Abel saw that it was a very beautiful place, and asked, "Daddy, why don't we live there?" "Well, son, we once did," Adam replied, "but your mother ate us out of house and home!"

It is an old story, a story of trees, a man and a woman, a garden, a serpent, rules kept and rules broken, and of God.

God formed a man, Adam, of the dust, and breathed life into him. God planted a garden, Eden, and made it beautiful with all things good. Among the many trees there, two were mentioned specifically. One was the tree of life; it was good for food, it was related to righteousness, and in the book of Revelation, to fellowship with God. The other tree was the tree of knowledge of good and evil (nowhere else in Holy Writ does this tree appear).

If we ask why such special attention is paid to these two trees, we have to finally say we don't know. God doesn't answer all of our questions — down here.

But this story is not so much interested in trees, as in the command of God concerning them. That's the serious part!

The Rules Are Simple

God gave Adam some rules to be obeyed, and they were very simple. He was to work and tend the trees of the garden (vs. 15), the fruit of the trees were to be eaten for food (vs. 16), and he was to stay away from one, just one of them — the tree of the knowledge of good and evil (vs. 17). God didn't tell Adam why, he just told him to *do* it! God still has rules for us to obey and expects total obedience from us.

Actually, there is nothing unusual about laws and rules. We live with them every day. We Americans have some 350,000 laws by which we must live. In 1980-81, there were some 1,500 new laws passed for us to live by. The IRS checks on us as do other law enforcement agencies in our country. We have reports to make, federal regulations to follow, rules upon rules to which we must conform. I know someone who wanted the "Remove Under Penalty of Law" tag off of her new mattress, but she was scared to do it because of the warning label.

So laws are not new to us, and our best judgment declares that we could not live happily without most of them. It is also true with the laws of God: We may protest them, we may proclaim them unfair, we may break them, but *in* or *out* of Eden, we humans are still expected to live on God's terms.

To honor the laws of God leads to our well-being. God is not a harsh despot who gives us difficult laws to obey just so he can frustrate us. Nor does God make rules for us to keep in order to assure that we remain subservient to him, lest we "become as God." What a stupid lie of the devil to think that God could ever be threatened in the least by puny humanity!

But for our *good*, God gives us rules; as a nation has laws for the common good, as a parent has rules for a child's protection, so God sets boundaries to insure our happiness. God knows that when we start trying to govern ourselves, apart from his direction, the result will be alienation and death. Freedom to enjoy life is always set in the prohibitions of God. Freedom comes from being bound to him. The Psalmist said (119:45), "I will keep thy law ... and I shall walk at liberty."

The Rules Are Broken

The serpent then enters the scene in the peaceful Garden of Eden. He begins to offer up possible alternatives to the ways of God. (vs. 3:1) He starts with a question which is craftily couched as a lie: "Really? You can't eat *any* of the fruit of the garden?" Eve's reply is, "Of course we can eat the fruit. It's just that one tree in the center that is off-limits. We eat that and we die!" Then the enemy of God and man calls God's truth a lie and declares, "You won't die!" The Big Lie of the devil is to practice talking theology about God rather than the performance of obedience. So the woman is convinced to break the laws of God, and then influences her husband to do the same.

So the story of Trust and Obedience to God turns into a lesson of Crime and Punishment. The freedom that seemed like slavery is exchanged for bondage and death.

We always become slaves when we disobey God. No bondage is worse than that wrought by sin! That's why Jesus said, "Ye shall know the Truth and the Truth will set you free."

Humans are always declaring their freedom, wishing for more "space," announcing that they belong only to "themselves." We want to be free from the enslavement of the kitchen, or from confinement of a job we don't like. Airplane companies claim to set us free, and Datsun says the same. There are deodorant companies which promise to set us free from the worry of underarm wetness and odor; a certain toothpaste declares we can be set free from dull teeth. Then we are promised freedom from pain by Tylenol, Excedrin, Bayer, and others. Other products play on our desperation for freedom by telling us we can be free from "ring-around-the-collar," and Lysol sets us free from germs. Our songs plaintively cry out our supreme desires in the refrains, "I want to be free" and "I did it *my* way." We want freedom to sleep at night with a clear conscience, freedom from fear of death, and above all, freedom from the terrors of the judgment day.

A teen-age boy told his parents he was going to run away from home. "Listen," he said, "I'm leaving home. There is nothing you can do to stop me. I want excitement, adventure, beautiful women, money, and fun. I'll never find it here, so I'm leaving. Just don't try to stop me!" As he headed for the door, his father leaped up and ran toward him. "Dad," the boy said firmly, "you heard what I said. Don't try to stop me. I'm going!" "Who's trying to stop you?" answered the father, "I'm going *with* you!"

But no matter what promises of "things-will-be-better-elsewhere" are made to us, we can never be truly free when we break the rules of God. It's disastrous.

Recall that God gave three rules about the trees in the Garden of Eden: Tend them, eat of them, and stay away from the tree of the knowledge of good and evil. We forget that Adam only broke one rule; the first two were completely acceptable to him. Adam didn't mind tending the trees; after all, that gave him something good to do and protected the means of his livelihood. He was very happy to eat of the fruit that God had so graciously provided. The third rule was just as important to his well-being as the first two, but he didn't *think* so. It remains true that the laws of God are given to keep us from falling into trouble and disaster. What a pity, that our willfulness against God causes us to enslave ourselves.

And now that the rule of God is broken, the captivity of Adam and Eve begins. Before, in the innocence of obedience to God, the husband and wife were together, naked, but unembarrassed and unashamed. Now, the broken law reveals their shame, their need of a covering. What they thought would be liberation turned out to be the beginning of fear and anxiety about themselves. It is always true that the power of guilt takes on its own destruction. Guilt causes us to jump when no one is there, to fear shadows, thinking they are some threatening reality. There is never any real security apart from obedience to God. TV ads may promise you will have financial security with certain money markets, that Prudential will be with you all the way, and that you are in "good hands with All-State" — but fine as all of these may be, the truth is that *nothing works* to make us secure when we break God's laws. When we reject him, separation and death result.

Christ Is God's Salvation for Us

With the realization of their disobedience upon their consciences, Adam and Eve could not bear to face God. So, as we often do, they hid from him. But the confrontation must come sooner or later, and it did for this pair. The goodness and mercy of God is shown when he (the betrayed) takes pity upon their shame and clothes them with animal skins (3:21). "And the Lord God made for Adam and for his wife garments of skins, and clothed them." This is an early portrait of God's New Testament Lamb who will die for the sins of the world.

All of us know what it is to try to hide our sins. They fester inside us. We try excusing ourselves, ignoring the sins, blaming others, hoping they will go away on their own — but still they have remained: black, dark, hopeless, ever pleading against us. Our sins reveal a naked soul, unclean and embarrassing in its ugliness.

But as we journey toward the cross this Lenten season, we are going to see that just as in the Eden story, an innocent victim will die to cover the guilty people. The holy, innocent, spotless, sinless Son of God dies to cover our sins with his own atoning, cleansing, covering blood. *He* will make amends for our disobedience!

A man who finally came to the knowledge of Christ as his own Saviour, said, "For years I ran from Jesus because I thought he was after me with a warrant for my arrest. I knew I had done wrong and deserved punishment. Then one day I discovered it wasn't a warrant for my arrest. It was a pardon for my sins!"

Then we learn that this narrative teaches the blessedness of bondage to the laws of God and also the freedom of choice to live, or not live, within those boundaries.

A society lady gave a gala garden party, and among the many guests were two ministers. She was standing by the punch bowl when the first reverend approached, looking thirsty. "I must tell you," she said to him, warningly, "the punch is spiked." "A little spirit never hurt anyone," he answered, filling his cup. The second minister approached. He got the same warning, drew himself up very piously, looked down his nose, and said, "I would rather commit adultery than drink an alcoholic beverage!" The first minister, aggravated by his judgmental attitude, snapped to attention and said, "I didn't realize I had a choice!"

We *always* have a choice. We don't have to serve God unless we choose. We can decide to obey or disobey, to live *in* or *out of* Eden. Christ's death is the justifying agent that restores Eden to us again, to the fellowship of God the Father.

So Choose — Blessed Bondage or Enslaving Freedom

Suppose Christ came to you today and said: "You don't have to follow me any longer. You no longer have to abide by the rules. You can forget all about Christian principles, you can do as *you* please, for a change. You don't have to get out of bed on Sunday mornings and go to church. You no longer have to make your decisions on the basis of right and wrong. You don't have to be careful to always speak the truth. You don't have to pay your pledges to the church. You don't have to tolerate the cantankerous people you don't like very well. You are free to be your own master."

Wouldn't you think it over and probably say to yourself, "No more conscience to guide me when I'm wrong, no more people in the family of God to care when I am in trouble, no one to rejoice with me, no where to go with my sins, no heaven, no hope, no life after death, no Christ to love me, no nothing . . ."

And then you and I would cry out, "No! No! No! Not that, Lord, anything but that! To whom would I go if I left you? I want to serve you. I will never, never, never choose to be free from this blessed bondage. I *like* being your slave. It's the only freedom I've ever known. I won't go free, I won't, I won't!"

Then, having made our choice, Christ would say,

"You mean it, you *really* mean it. Till death then, you will be my slave till death?"

And we would reply humbly, thankfully, honestly, surely, "Yes, indeed I choose life with God rather than my own will and way. I will serve you. I will obey you. I will worship and adore you — till death — and beyond death into life eternal!"

Small wonder that we still love to sing George Matheson's great hymn:

"Make me a captive, Lord
And then I shall be free."

3
Faith Isn't Easy — But It Works!

Second Sunday in Lent
Genesis 12:1-8

Now the Lord said to Abram, "Go from your country and your kindred and your father's house to the land that I will show you. And I will make of you a great nation, and I will bless you, and make your name great, so that you will be a blessing. I will bless those who bless you, and him who curses you, I will curse; and by you all the families of the earth shall bless themselves."

So Abram went, as the Lord had told him; and Lot went with him. Abram was seventy-five years old when he departed from Haran. And Abram took Sarai his wife, and Lot his brother's son, and all their possessions which they had gathered, and the persons that they had gotten Haran; and they set forth to go to the land of Canaan. When they had come to the land of Canaan, Abram passed through the land to the place of Shechem, to the oak of Moreh. At that time the Canaanites were in the land. Then the Lord appeared to Abram, and said, "To your descendants I will give this land." So be built there an altar to the Lord, who had appeared to him. Thence he removed to the mountain on the east of Bethel, and pitched his tent, with Bethel on the west and Ai on the east; and there he built an altar to the Lord and called on the name of the Lord.

A mother who was busy cooking supper in the kitchen asked her five-year-old son to go down to the basement and get her a can of chicken soup. The little boy didn't want to go alone, and he said, "Mommy, it's dark down there, and I'm scared." "It's all right,

Johnny," she said, "you go on down and get that soup for me. I need it for this recipe." Then she continued, as she saw his hesitation, "Besides, Jesus will be there with you, now go and get me that soup!" Johnny went down the stairs, slowly opened the basement door, and peeked inside. It was darker than a sack of black cats, and he was scared. His hands began to tremble, but then he got an idea. He said, "Jesus, if you're in there, please hand me a can of chicken soup!"

An over-active imagination often makes us fear to walk by faith rather than by sight. Our text makes it clear that faith isn't easy — but it works!

Abraham has been briefly introduced in the chapter preceding our text. We know only that his father was Terah, his wife was Sarai, and that she was barren. Then we are told that Abraham and Sarai, his nephew Lot, and Terah left the place of their birth in Ur of the Chaldees, and settled in Haran. In Ur they had been sun-worshipers, but in Haran, God (Yahweh) spoke to Abraham and gave him some unbelievable promises.

The Promises and the Promiser — (verses 1-3)

There is no promise without a Promise-maker. Who the promiser is makes all the difference in the world as to how we regard the promise. When someone issues an order or gives information or states a promise, our first reaction is to inquire: "*Who* says so?" It's hard to have faith in persons who are untrustworthy. Unlike Nixon aide Charles Colson, Liddy did not turn religious during his time in prison. A few days after his release from prison for his part in the Watergate scandal, Liddy said, "I found within myself all I need and all I ever shall need. I am a man of great faith, but my faith is in George Gordon Liddy. I have never failed me." Because of his part in the wrong-doing that unsettled our nation, we would have problems having faith in a man like that. Once a person has failed to be trustworthy, we don't want to put our confidence in him. If someone reneges on a promise, breaks a commitment, or tells us a lie, we doubt that person thereafter. If we find that someone has played false with us, we question all that person says or does. But God, the Promiser in this text, *cannot* lie, and not one of his good promises has ever been known to fail. We trust the promise because of the Promise-maker.

Even though the promises seem outlandish and impossible to fulfill, Abraham trusts them because he feels he can trust the God who made them. That's what faith is all about. Faith in a doubtful promiser is foolishness, but faith knows that the Word of God is dependable, and to base one's trust in his sure, true Word is to stand on solid rock.

It has been reported that there are some 33,000 promises in the Bible that God has made to his people. Would we not be wise to find the ones that apply to our present needs and situation and claim them for ourselves in the name of our Faithful Promiser?

No matter how fool-hardy it seems, God can always be trusted. These promises to Abraham are new and fresh, encompassing not only Abraham and his future, but even the future of the outsiders. They were "too good to be true," but Abraham believed them anyway! God promised so *much:* well-being, security, prosperity, and prominence. And the well-being of Abraham carried also the possibility for the well-being of other nations. How good of God to extend the promised blessings to include the larger view! God never intended any of us to live in a vacuum of selfishness. We must always live with, for, and among others — "By you shall all of the families of the earth be blessed."'

And all of these wondrous things because "THE

LORD SAID." If we can only get a "thus saith the Lord" for our lives, all will be well! Then we'll sing with new meaning and fervor:

"Standing on the promises of Christ my King,
Thro' eternal ages let His praises ring;
Glory in the highest, I will shout and sing,
Standing on the promises of God!"

The Pilgrimage — (verses 4-6)

Suppose Abraham had chosen to stay in Haran? Remember, Sarai was barren — they had no children, no promise, no future. True, leaving Haran meant risk, but it also meant hope. Abraham heard God's call — accepted, embraced, and believed his promise — and WENT! He obeyed, asking no questions! How often we question the command of God. How easily Abraham might have asked, as we often do: "God, are you sure you mean me?" — "God, it's never been done before, has it?" — "Why me, God?" — "Aren't you asking too much?" — "It's pretty risky, isn't it?"

Abraham believed the promise of God when there was no visible evidence. And that's the definition of faith, according to Hebrews 11:1: "Now faith is the assurance of things hoped for, the conviction of things not seen." Faith always sees the invisible, believes the incredible, and receives the impossible.

Abraham, then, becomes the prototype of all disciples and Christians who forsake everything and follow Christ." Peter said to Jesus, "Lo, we have left everything and followed you." Note that it was certainly far from easy for Abraham to obey God, nor was it ever promised to be a rose garden. Claiming and following a promise requires a big decision and often a radical repentance, and repentance is never easy for stubborn humankind. Faith is always a battle.

Occasionally you hear someone say, "Well, it *must* be the will of God for me to do this, for it all worked out so beautifully." That's poor theology, for the devil can make things work well for you too, if it serves his evil purpose. We must always watch whose banner we follow. "Easy" doesn't make it right, and difficulty doesn't mean that God has forsaken or forgotten you. We might well remember that the brightest lightning comes from the blackest clouds, and the purest faith comes from life's hardest trials.

It must have been very stressful and exceedingly arduous for Abraham to obey the leading of God as he attempted to walk by faith in the Promise-maker. It meant having no roots, being on-the-go, and wandering from place to place. My John and I have a dear friend who is a United Methodist pastor, and therefore a part of the church's itinerant system. One day our preacher-friend, Hal Brady, gathered his three children around him and told them the bishop was sending them from the First United Methodist Church in Alpharetta, Georgia, to the First United Methodist Church of Carrollton, Georgia. After he had explained it all to them, Hal finally asked, "How do you feel about it?" Jason, the youngest Brady boy, answered with his usual unruffled attitude, "Dad, I was born to move!" So were *we* born to move — and so was Abraham. The text uses the metaphor of a journey as a way of picturing the life of faith. Abraham went from Haran to Canaan — and there we see his pilgrimage leading him from the northern shrines of Shechem and Bethel, then south to the Negev and to Hebron — always trusting the promise. He was a pilgrim and a sojourner, achieving the fulfillment of the promise in part, but only a step at a time. It must have been a good life, as life always is when we obey the commands of God — but far from an easy one.

Christian disciples are known as followers of "the Way." "The Way" is the way of Jesus: the way of persecution, the way of the cross, the way of suffering, even the way of death. We follow the promises of a God who ever leads us. He directs our path in his Kingdom, a kingdom of peace and justice and freedom. Often our pilgrimage takes us where the community of faith is scorned and despised. We are at odds with the world; our principles are different than those around us; we are often misunderstood and not always accepted. But we, too, are strangers and pilgrims, having here no continuing city, but we seek a heaven, yet to be given to us.

That's why the promise is often difficult to believe and to practice. We are set in the midst of those who march to another drummer, who claim their way is "easier," "more sophisticated," "more fun," "not so rigid." We are a minority, accused of living in a fantasy world, of seeing things that aren't there. In truth, we *do* see him who is invisible, carrying always before our eyes of faith the standard of his blood-stained cross. That's what Lent is all about — we "follow in his train."

But how can we be a blessing to the outsiders (in Abraham's case, the Canaanites) unless we hold fast to our faith in the Promise of the One whose Word is unshakable? Don't forget that Abraham and Sarai, the barren ones, are on their way to fruitfulness. This is a paradigm of the resurrection. Paul speaks of the resurrection when he mentions the God in whom Abraham believed. That means, then, that we followers of the Promiser get to experience life out of death, too, and bring it to those who are yet dead in their sins.

Christian faith is first and always a centered, personal act of trust and commitment, always founded in Jesus Christ our Savior. Out of our right relationship with God, we extend our faith to include our neighbors and the world. The sure trust and confidence that Christ died for *my* sins, that he loves *me*, and that he accepts *me*, gives me such a life of blessing that it overflows to those around. So, like Abraham, because we are blessed, we can be a blessing!

The Precious Presence — (verses 7-8)

No matter how faithful the Promise-maker, nor how marvelous the promises, we could not live without a sense of the precious presence of God in our lives. I have a special "Missouri friend," Dr. Arnold Prater, who loves God as deeply as anyone I know. One morning, in a phone call, I said to him, "Arnold, how are you?" His answer was a gem. He responded, "Oh, I'm fine. I woke up this morning and Jesus nearly smothered me with his Presence!" That's what Abraham needed, that's what we can't live without. So, wherever Abraham went, he built an altar. People of faith can afford to do no less. God was Abraham's center. From God he received directives for the journey and strength for their accomplishment.

That's why worship must always be at the center of our pilgrimage. We go to church to worship God, not primarily for fellowship with others, as fine as that may be. Henry Ward Beecher had to be absent from Plymouth Church one Sunday. His brother preached for him. The church auditorium was crowded, but when it was evident that the eloquent Henry Ward Beecher was not going to appear, many started to leave the church. The brother of the great man was not at all disturbed. Calling for silence, he said, "All who came this morning to worship Henry Ward Beecher may leave now. The rest will remain to worship God." After that, no one left.

Let us never disparage the value of seeing our friends at worship, but that is secondary to what is of prime importance. Harry Golden, the wonderful storyteller, tells of a time when he was young and asked his father, "If you don't believe in God, why do you go to synagogue so regularly?" His father answered, "Jews go to synagogue for all sorts of reasons. My friend Garfinkle, who is Orthodox, goes to talk to God. I go to talk to Garfinkle."

Abraham's calling on Yahweh's name means he had decided to cling to no one but the Promiser. Even among the "unbelievers" (the Canaanites), his altar was a sign that it is God alone who is trusted. It was a refutation of all their gods and idols. The altar symbolized God's presence and the place where he met him for conversation. Now we, many years later, the followers of "the Way," build and make altars wherever we go, to call on the name of the Lord. Sometimes at that altar, we praise and adore the Promise-maker; other times we passionately entreat and petition him, and then still other times we offer sacrifices of self and substance in thanksgiving to him — but in it all, we turn in simple, child-like, trusting faith to our God and to no other! His Presence is our certainty that the fulfilled promise is on the way!

Faith Works — So Don't Lose It!

A tender story is told of a seventy-nine-year-old lady by the name of Mrs. Harriet Hudson. She didn't have many material things, but she did own six precious things, until a tornado roared through her tiny, crudely built house. She had a coat, which had been given to her by her now deceased husband. It was only imitation fur, but it was a Christmas gift and very precious to her. Another of her treasures was a stove, which was destroyed when the chimney fell on it. She'd cooked many a meal on it, and she loved that " 'namel wood range." Then there was a faded picture.

It was of her father, "the reverend of the Methodist Church." She also had an old, decrepit organ, but the wind took it too. She loved to play the hymns on it, and even though it was thirty years old, it was the "crownin' glory" of the house. Her Bible that had all the names and birthdays and deaths and weddings in it was blown away. But when Mrs. Hudson totaled all the losses of her home and recalled the things she had cherished that had gone to the four winds, she just closed her eyes, clasped her hands as if in prayer, and said, "The Lord giveth, the Lord taketh away, blessed be the name of the Lord." The story says that the Red Cross came and helped out, but of course could not restore to her the coat, the stove, the picture, the organ, nor her Bible. When someone asked her why God would take all her things from her, she, in simple and beautiful faith, replied, I don't *s'posed* to know why I trust him!" That's one thing the tornado didn't get — her sixth precious thing — her FAITH!

4
Midnight Turned Into High Noon

Third Sunday in Lent
Isaiah 42:14-21

". . . I will turn the darkness before them into light . . ."

David Hume, the philospher, once wrote an essay on the sufficiency of the light of nature for man's spiritual matters. About the same time, F. W. Robertson, a noted minister, published a sermon upholding the opposite thesis, pointing out that the light of nature needs to be supplemented by the light of a revelation from God. Mutual friends of the philosopher and preacher decided to bring the two together to debate the matter. When the evening ended, Hume rose to leave. Robertson took a light to show him the way, but Hume protested, saying, "Don't worry about me. I always find the light of nature sufficient." But when he opened the door, he stumbled over something on the steps and fell headlong into the street. The minister jumped down beside the prostrate philosopher and held a light over him to see that he wasn't hurt; then he softly but firmly said, "You *do* need a little light from above."

God knew that we humans would need light from above, too, otherwise we'd stumble around forever in darkness without his illumination, so he sent Christ to be that light. Christ left the brilliance of heaven to come to a dismal and dark world. It was a world so dark his own did not even recognize nor accept him. He endured the darkness of prejudice, intolerance, selfishness and hatred. It was night in the upper room when the disciples met for the Last Supper. It was black night in the Garden of Gethsemane when he sweat great drops of blood. It was night when one of his own betrayed him. It was during the night that he was shuffled all night from one unjust trial to another. And when they finally crucified the Light of the World, the sun refused to shine, and it was midnight in the middle of the day. What a dark night of the soul for the Savior!

But now, the cross on which he died is so wondrously illuminated that even the hymns of the cross fairly glow with its brightness:

"When the woes of life o'er take me,
Hopes deceive and fears annoy,
Never shall the cross forsake me:
Lo! it *glows* with peace and joy."

or

"Above the hills of time the cross is *gleaming*,
Fair as the *sun* when night has turned to *day;*
And from it love's pure *light* is richly streaming,

To cleanse the heart, and banish sin away."

The context comes out of the setting where the prophet describes the last years of the Babylonian exile with all of the disaster that had befallen Israel as the unavoidable consequence of sin and disobedience. But the proclamation here is the good news that Israel's salvation is coming, and that it will encompass all of nature and all nations. The text, "I will turn the darkness before them into light," signifies in mythical language the radical reversal which the salvation of God always brings. For us who live on this side of Christ's coming, that "darkness into light" is always realized in the cross. Paul said, "For God, who commanded the light to shine out of darkness, hath shined in our hearts, to give the light of the knowledge of the glory of God in the face of Jesus Christ." (2 Corinthians 4:6 KJV)

Most of us relate very well to the dark night of the soul. We have all been there, and we long for the light. It is no figment of the imagination that Christ's cross has the power to change the darkness of our human condition to the brightness of noon day.

The Condition of Difficulty

The dark condition of some of you today is that you have so many problems that you can't imagine there would ever be light again in your life. No solution is visible. You are troubled with financial difficulties, or maybe marital problems cast gloom about you, perhaps the problem is a sickness that gives you no relief, or maybe the sun is obscured because of the death of a loved one. Life has tumbled in around you. In a *Peanuts* cartoon strip, there is a conversation between Lucy and Charlie Brown. Lucy said that life was like a deck chair. Some place it so they can see where they are going, some place it so they can see where they have been, and some place it so they can see where they are at the present. Charlie Brown replies, "I can't even get mine unfolded!" That's precisely where many of you are. Life is so filled with difficulties that you can't find a way to put it back together again.

Others of you are persuaded that you are all alone in your difficulties. The nineteenth century actor, E. A. Sothern, was watching a small boy one day. The child wanted to go outdoors to join his playmates, but feared they would not accept him. The actor wanted to cheer him up, so he took him by the hand and said, playfully, "Let's hide behind the curtain and they won't know where we are!" The boy looked at him disconsolately and said, "Suppose they don't care?" God *does* care about you and the path you tread that seems so devoid of light. Do you think that for a moment, you, his child, could ever have a problem that God, in his own good time, could not sweep out of the way? And if your difficulty must remain, he will certainly lead you over it or help you bear it.

A visitor to the chapel at the Lutheran Seminary in Guntur, India, noticed the unusual height of the altar. He had never seen an altar that was shoulder-high. The guide explained: "Haven't you noticed that along the roads of India, ever so often there are great rocks of this height? When travelers, carrying heavy burdens, come upon such a rock, they can slide the burden from their shoulders onto the rock and sit down in its shade to rest awhile. A shoulder-high altar, then, reminds the worshiper that God is our Resting Rock. When we are exhausted with the problems, God is our burden-bearer and our light for the way.

Ernie Pyle, the famous war correspondent of World War II, wrote to a friend, "If you have any light, shine it in my direction. God knows that I have run out of light." If you, too, have run out of light, look and see Christ silhouetted on his cross against the dark, threatening skyline of your life, and dawn will illuminate your days!

The Condition of Depression

Has a dream just crumbled before your eyes, shattering into a million pieces? Are you so low and depressed you can hardly see the next step you should take? Is gloom a heavy cloud that follows you wherever you go and whatever you do? Do blinding tears make you stumble and fall?

Nearly everyone knows the blackness of depression now and then. According to the National Institute of Mental Health, between six and eight million Americans suffer from severe depression. People like Beethoven, Tchaikovsky, Tolstoy, and Abraham Lincoln suffered from depression. Two of the best preachers of this century, Harry Emerson Fosdick and J. Wallace Hamilton, fought depression. Winston Churchill waged a life-long battle against depression, which he called, "My black dog." Who of us has not known negative feelings, "blue days," and occasions of despair?

The distinguished missionary, E. Stanley Jones, in his classic book, *The Christ of the Indian Road,* tells how in his early days in India he was prostrated with illness and depression. One day, in Lucknow, he turned into a church to pray, and there he heard a voice saying, "Are you ready for the work to which I have called you?" "No, Lord," he replied. "I'm done for. I've reached the end of my resources and I can't go on." "Then," said the voice, "if you will turn the problem over to me and not worry about it, I will take care of it." "Lord," was Brother Jones' eager reply, "I close the bargain right here." Then he rose from his knees, knowing that he was healed of the depression and gloom, possessed with life and hope and peace, because "He is able!" Now, my friend, *that* is light of the best kind!

A glimpse of Love on a Cross-tree puts the mists to flight. Put your heart and your hurt and your hand in the nail-scarred hands of Christ. He *allows* (not sends) things that seem evil to you sometimes, but it is only so he can weave them into a pattern for your blessedness.

The Condition of Doubt

Sometimes we are absolutely overwhelmed with spiritual doubts. Is there any great darkness than the shadow cast by doubt? And no matter how hard we try, we can't seem to keep the doubts and questions from coming to us: questions of God, doubts and fears of heaven, of hell, even of our salvation. They plague us when we least expect them, rearing their ugly heads just when we think we have at long-last conquered them. But, you cannot *make* yourself believe! Martin Luther, great saint and believer that he was, often struggled to have faith in a gracious God. He obeyed all the laws and rituals of the church. He afflicted his body by lying naked on the cold floor of his monk's cell all night. He fasted until he fainted for lack of food. He confessed his sins for six hours at a stretch. But in spite of all this, doubts plagued him, and once he said, "For more than a week I was close to the very gates of death and hell. I trembled in all my members. Christ was wholly lost to me. I was shaken by desperation and blasphemy of God." But Luther, as you and I must and will, worked through it till he was able to say, "Whenever the devil comes to test me, and to fill me with doubts of my salvation, when I am tempted to believe I am no good, and that

God would not have me, then I crawl by faith, on my hands and knees, back to the baptismal font, and there I recall that God in Christ did accept me and make me his own dear child."

Doubts come to great saints and to people like ourselves, but that does not mean we are lost forever in the night of our distrust. Our unbelief can change to radiant faith. When Michael Faraday, the great scientist, lay dying, a friend asked him, "What are your speculations?" Gently, Faraday replied, "Speculations? I have none. I know Whom I have believed. I rest my soul upon certainties!"

Dark demons of doubt cannot live in Calvary's radiance! St. Martin of Tours was seated in his cell when a knock came at the door, and a lordly presence entered. "Who are you?" asked the saint, and the figure replied, "I am the Savior." The saint was suspicious and asked, "Where are the print of the nails?" — and the devil vanished. So, for our lives, the demons of doubt disappear when we look at the lustre that shines from the cross. When we see Jesus, hanging on that tree, his blazing love reveals verities to us, drives our doubts and fears into oblivion, just as the morning fog dissipates in the rising of the sun.

The Condition of Defeat (of sin)

The biggest problem that most of us face is the defeat from the sin(s) that so easily beset us. We've tried to hide our sins, ignore them, disown them, blame them on someone else, but still they refuse to go away. We've been conquered by them so many times that we wonder if there is the slightest possibility of our ever winning through. When we are honest with what we are, in the sight of a holy God, we admit that we have not done well. The story is told of a mother who found her young son standing before the bathroom mirror. There were tears rolling down his cheeks. Alarmed and sympathetic, she asked, "What's wrong? What's the matter? Why are you crying?" The boy replied, "I just don't like the way I turned out!"

Dissatisfaction with our wrongdoing makes us keenly aware that confession is called for. We need to admit we are in darkness and have lost our way. However big and black and condemning our sins are, they need to be laid open to the searchlight of God, as we declare our sinfulness.

Bishop Paul Duffey tells of a man who went to confession and wanted the priest to absolve him of his sins. The Father said, "All right, son, what have you done?" The man replied, "I've taken some lumber that did not belong to me." The priest responded, "Well, that's not too bad. You put $5.00 in the offering plate and see that you never steal lumber again." The man said, "All right, Father, but it *was* quite a bit of lumber." "Was it enough to build a bird house?" the priest asked. "Yes," the culprit admitted. "Then you'd better put $10.00 in the offering and say ten 'Hail Marys.'" "O.K.," the man said, "but it was *quite* a lot of lumber." "Enough to build a garage?" queried the priest. "Yes," confessed the penitent. "In that case, you'd better put $25.00 in the offering and say fifty 'Hail Marys.'" "All right, Father, but it was still a bit more than that," the sinner responded. "Well," said the priest, "You'd better make a novena (a Roman Catholic nine days' devotion.)" "All right, Father," said the man. "I don't know what a novena is, but if you've got the plans, I've sure got the lumber!"

But it is really no laughing matter when we realize our only chance of victory over the dark defeat of our sinning is through Jesus Christ and the atoning grace of his cross. There is no question but that we all need liberation from sin. The sins of the rich are not always the same as the sins of the poor, the sins of the

Christian may be different from those of the Hindu or Buddhist, but the needs of humankind are all essentially the same — we need forgiveness! Unless we confess it plainly, we are simply betraying the truth of the Gospel and missing the chance of freedom from our wrongs.

Robert Louis Stevenson, as a small boy, loved to watch the old lamp lighter go down the street. One night he said to his nurse, "Look, that man is putting holes in the darkness." That is exactly what happens to us when we survey the cross — the Divine Luminary hanging there stabs life's murky gloom and sin's midnight with the high noon of forgiveness! God's radical X-ray, his laser beam of love, burns our sins away, shrivels them into nothingness in the brightness of Calvary's glorious and resplendent light.

So sin *is* my dark trouble, but God's light is Christ who died to show me my worst enemy — ME! — my sinful, treacherous, wicked self — and now that self has been to the cross and seen the light and darkness is no more! The refrain to the Lenten hymn, "Alas! And Did My Savior Bleed?" shouts the same message:

"At the cross, at the cross, where I first saw the *light!*
And the burden of my heart rolled away —
It was there by faith I received my *sight,*
And now I am happy all the *day!*"

Midnight Turned Into High Noon!

The *Charlotte Observer* gave an account sometime back of a cab driver who had driven a city taxi for many years and had become a pretty good judge of people. One Christmas, one of his fares looked to be a desperate man. He asked to be taken to the corner of Providence and Queens roads and then commanded the cabbie to stop. Then he just sat there, for a long time, with the meter running. The man said nothing, just sat staring. The next night the incident was repeated. The third night it happened again — the man just asked the taxi driver to take him to the same location, and he paid the bill that accrued while he simply sat and stared and said nothing. The man seemed desperate and pathetic. But then the cab driver happened to notice that there were a supermarket and a drug store across the way, and he thought there must be a lot of cash in there during the busy Christmas season. Maybe his far was casing the place for a big robbery. So, he said to the man in the back seat of the cab, "I need some cigarettes, I'll be right back." While he was in one of the stores, he called the police and told them what was going on. The police got there in a big hurry and asked the silent man in the cab why he sat night after night at this particular corner. The man pointed to the window of the Myers Park United Methodist Church, a gorgeous, beautifully back-lighted stained glass window. He said, "I never had much religion. I don't even know how to pray. My wife is very sick, and the hospital tells me she's real bad. But then I found this window. Something about its light gives me strength and peace, and somehow looking at it I have the words to pray."

That's a pretty fair description of what has happened to us. In our helplessness and darkness, in the midnight of the soul, we have felt hopeless, desperate, despairing, and lost. Then, piercing the black gloom of our night, has been the window of God. We've looked at the cross, shining against the backdrop of our night, and its light has given us strength and peace, and we, too, have learned to pray again! That's really turning midnight into high noon!

5

Returning: Real or Ruse?

Fourth Sunday in Lent
Hosea 5:15-6:1

"I will return again to my place, until they acknowledge their guilt and seek my face, and in their distress they see me, saying, 'Come, let us return to the Lord; for he has torn, that he may heal us; he has stricken, and he will bind us up.'"

A woman was filling out an employment application. When she came to the line marked "age," she hesitated a long time. Finally, the personnel manager leaned across his desk and whispered to her, "The longer you wait, the worse it gets!"

That's true of repentance and returning to God, too. The longer you put it off, the harder it is to do it.

Hosea, in the context and in this text, uses bold images of God — he pictures God as a ravaging lion and even as a man who absents himself from his disobedient people. He withdraws from those worshipers who thought he could be used for their own selfish purposes, thinking that they could treat God however expediency dictated.

The point is, of course, not that God is *really* absent, but because they had rejected him and his claims upon them, he let them suffer the fate of *their own choosing.* So, the Lord will withdraw himself from them until they recognize their guilt, return to him, seek his presence, and turn honestly and sincerely to him in their distress. They must realize that the power of God is not available to them for selfish exploitation.

The words in the next verse, then, (Hosea 6:1) indicate the response that God longs for: "Come, let us return to the Lord." With bold faith, the people turn for healing to the very One who wounded them! God the Chastiser is also God the Healer. There is only one God. There is no chance, then, of their making an appeal to a second deity against the righteous claims of the one, nor is there need for such an appeal. There is also a clear recognition of guilt here, and an awareness of God's judgment — but also a sight of the love and healing power of the Lord! But it all hinges on their "Returning" — it's a good decision they are making.

But there are two ways of returning. There can be a

Returning Without Repentance

Was their ready returning an easy hope that God would immediately restore them to their former prosperity? Were they hoping they could wallow in their selfish excesses again? Were they truly sorry for their sins, or only sorry because they had been caught? Was their repentance a result of reaping the pain and wrath their actions had brought down upon their heads, or because they deplored having injured a holy God? Was it all just a "wordy" ruse to escape judgment for their sins, and hopefully they could still live as they jolly well pleased?

The aim of Israel was not really to return to the Lord, but to remove the inconvenience that God's anger had caused them. Their concern was to "get what they could" from a rich and powerful God.

A man went to an old friend to ask for a loan of some money. He didn't have any collateral, and he didn't want to be charged any interest. The friend said he didn't think their friendship was close and binding enough to justify such a claim upon it, and so he refused to make the loan. "But, John," the man said, "how can you say that, how can you refuse me? We grew up together. I helped you make it through school. I even saved you from drowning once. I helped you get started in business. I persuaded my cousin to marry your sister. I can't believe you'd say we were not close enough for you to make me a loan!" "Oh," replied John, "I remember you did all of those things for me. What bothers me is, what have you done for me *lately?*" Such is the ingratitude of those who only make a ruse of repentance. The kind of repentance that is only wily subterfuge won't do! God won't accept it. God's love, mercy, and grace are unlimited, but our desire for his grace must at least be honest and sincere.

We can't pass over our sinning so lightly. This attitude is reminiscent of St. Augustine who prayed, "Lord, forgive my sins — but not yet!" It is said that another time he prayed, "Lord, forgive my sins" — and after a pause — "except one." The anguish in St. Augustine's soul is revealed in his confession, "How often have I lashed at my will and cried, 'Leap now! Leap now!' — and even as I said it, crouched for the leap, and all but leaped — and yet I did not leap — and the life to which I was accustomed held me more than the life for which I truly yearned."

Our desperate need, in our returning to the Lord, is for a heart that, without deceit, calls for forgiveness. The media reported some months ago that a Park Avenue plastic surgeon, Dr. Peter Fodor, had offered a new face to Jean Harris, who is serving a fifteen-year-sentence for killing Scarsdale Diet Developer, Dr. Herman Tarnower. Fodor said a new visage would help Ms. Harris face her prison term with a better outlook. I do not discount the value of the "lift" that physical rejuvenation may bring, but for the most part, our need is not external, but internal. A new heart would help us more than a new face!

We, today, are not too different, in our coming to God, from the people of Hosea's day. True, we are uncomfortable when we sin, but we pass over it very casually, lightly, and flippantly, with a bored, "Whoops! Sorry about that, God!" We give God not a full repentance but our "almost."

Tragically, this is true with us as individuals and as the body of Christ when we meet for corporate worship. We are far more taken with celebration than with confession. A survey reported that eighty-seven percent of the Sunday morning services in the United Methodist Church have no confession of sins. In the Lutheran Church in America, which for centuries has made confession a mandatory and vital part of the service, the confession is now "optional."

It is frightening when our sins, done to a holy God, no longer disturb, worry, or frighten us. *The St. Petersburg Times* reported that a man was on trial for the murder of an elderly woman. The attorney was pleading for his life, and the accused was fighting to stay awake. His actions were described: "The eyes closed, opened, closed again. Every time the lids came down, they stayed shut a little longer!" How can you possibly be charged with killing an eighty-one-year-old woman and doze off at your murder trial? But, the devil infects you and me with the same slumbering insensitivity to the wrongs that we do, and we figure we don't "need" to be troubled with a guilty conscience. It takes the "joy out of life," so why don't we just get on with celebration?

We affirm that we "feel good about ourselves" and about God — and claim we feel "close to Jesus." All of this is fine, but, nevertheless, the measure of authentic repentance, returning, and revival is always manifest in our godly sorrow for sin and in the resultant change in the quality of one's life. It is certainly true that the church is the place for sinners, but not for sinners who are determined to remain sinners, and not for obstinate sinners who have no regrets over their sins and no intention other than to remain in them. One could almost say, "Unless we change, we have not really returned!"

Returning for Radical Change

Bishop Dana Dawson was once called to a church to receive a group of young people into the church. It was time for the confirmation, and the bishop asked the question: "Will you renounce the devil and all his works?" The young lad standing in front of Dawson was so over-awed he just looked at him. The bishop repeated the question, but still no response from the child. Finally, Dawson said once more: "Will you renounce the devil and all his works?" Then he whispered, "Say, 'I will,' if you will." The boy then in a loud voice exclaimed, "I will if you will!" That's what real repentance and returning is; it is going for "broke" if one truly returns to God.

I preached a revival at the Wilmington Island United Methodist Church in Savannah, Georgia, recently. The meeting closed the day before St. Patrick's Day. It is a memorable experience to be in Savannah for the Big Day of the Irish! They go as "all out" in Savannah as they do on the "old sod." They've been known to paint the dome of the City Hall green. The Savannah River is colored green. "Honorary Irish" buttons are handed out to the poor souls who can claim no kin nor blood with the Irish. Grits are green, and even beer is green! No matter what the uninitiated and the non-Irish think of the day and its customs, you cannot help but be impressed with their radical allegiance to their Irish blood. I reveled in my own Irish ancestry and fought the smugness that comes of the knowledge that the heritage was mine! Returning to God should be just that same kind of "all out" determination! It should be born of an extreme and urgent awareness of need of his pardon.

Human hearts are fickle, and we are capable of turning again and again away from God — and to a disregarding of his laws. How marvelous to know that the mercy of God is always available! But healing and renewal have lasting effects only when they are sustained by solid commitment. Then, and perhaps *only* then, do we begin to live as "changed" persons. A dear friend, Dr. John Strohman, told of a new Christian who went back to work for the first time after he had been converted. One of the workers, who had heard of his confession, decided to test him and try out his new-found faith. He said: "I hear you got religion?" "Yes, I did," the new convert responded. "So now you are a Christian?" the trouble-maker persisted. "That's right," the new Christian affirmed. "I suppose you now believe the Bible?" "Yes, sir, I do." The man continued to test the new convert by asking, "That means you believe all that stuff about Jesus walking on water, healing sick people, and what about turning all that water into wine? Can you believe that?" The man said, "Yes, sir, I believe all that. I don't find it too hard to believe when I found that God has changed an alcoholic like me into a sober man, a liar into an honest man, and my wife and children into a family that's no longer afraid of me when I come home. Yes, if Jesus can do all that, then I think I can handle the story of water into wine!"

Returning, of course, is always an individual decision, but evidence of our returning is manifested in our relationships. We come to see that in the wider sense, our lives are bound up with all the people of God. There are no limits to this bond. We can never disassociate ourselves in our relationship with God from our relationships with others. Hence, in our corporate worship, we sense the fellowship of all of God's family. In Holy Communion, we partake with a world-wide, heaven-included community of saints. In our prayers, we pray not only for our own needs, but the needs of the community of faith, the nation, and the world. The clearer our vision of God, the wider our vision of his world! The more genuine our reason for "returning," the larger the scope of our loving. Love is never static and mechanical, but dynamic and personal. Devotion to Christ is normally inseparable from devotion to people, for Christ is a people-lover and a people-carer!

God, in his love, requires us to love others. God is willing to forgive us, but EXPECTS us to live in mutual love and caring with others. Ritual repentance is easy, superficial sorrow is simple, but radical change is hard, and loving and obeying is tough and vital!

God's Nearness in Repentance

There are those who would presume upon a good God by saying he is "ALL LOVE" — and that he is! But God is also "ALL JUSTICE," as the Prophet Hosea (and Amos and Isaiah and others) reminds us. God let the nation and his people decide as to what their fate would be. He still does the same for us. God NEVER sends anyone to hell. His eternally extended love would not allow that — but, if we "choose" that destiny, though it breaks his heart, he will still let us decide.

An American Indian was converted to Christianity and went back to his reservation to share his faith. In explaining salvation by grace alone, he found an earthworm and put it in the middle of a circle of dried leaves. Then he set the leaves afire all around the edge. The worm tried to escape but ran into fire whatever way he went. Finally, maybe instinctively knowing the situation was hopeless, he crawled back to the center, went limp, resigned to die. At this point, the Indian convert reached down and plucked the worm from the flame and said to the people: "This is what it means to be saved. When we abandon all efforts to save ourselves, God comes to save us." This is exactly what God's great and wondrous grace, vividly portrayed in Lent's cross, does for us. It is the super-Divine attempt of God to entice us to choose to return in radical repentance to him and live! And that cross on Golgotha's brow reminds us that God can never again be absent from our world. He comes so close to each of us in the atoning death of his Son that in touching us with that precious blood, we are made clean and whole. A ruse at repentance is to be lost. Real repentance and faith is to realize God is nearer to us than hands and feet and breathing!

6

God Can't Keep a Good Secret!

Fifth Sunday in Lent
Ezekiel 37:1-3 (4-10) 11-14

The hand of the Lord was upon me, and he brought me out by the Spirit of the Lord, and he set me down in the midst of the valley; it was full of bones. And he led me round among them; and behold, there were very many upon the valley; and lo, they were very dry. And he said to me, "Son of man, can these bones live?" And I answered, "O Lord God, thou knowest." Again he said to me, "Prophesy to these bones, and say to them, O dry bones, hear the word of the Lord. Thus says the Lord God to these bones: Behold, I will cause breath to enter you, and you shall live. And I will lay sinews upon you, and will cause flesh to come upon you, and cover you with skin, and put breath in you, and you shall live; and you shall know that I am the Lord."

So I prophesied as I was commanded; and as I prophesied, there was a noise, and behold, a rattling; and the bones came together, bone to bone. And as I looked, there were sinews on them, and flesh had come upon them, and skin had covered them; but there was no breath in them. Then he said to me, "Prophesy to the breath, prophesy, son of man, and say to the breath, Thus says the Lord God: Come from the four winds, O breath, and breathe upon these slain, that they may live." So I prophesied as he commanded me, and the breath came into them, and they lived, and stood upon their feet, an exceedingly great host.

Then he said to me, "Son of man, these bones are the whole house of Israel. Behold, they say, 'Our bones are dried up and our hope is lost; we are clean cut off.' Therefore prophesy, and say to them, Thus says the Lord God: Behold, I will open your graves, O my people; and I will bring you home into the land of Israel. And you shall know that I am the Lord, when I open your graves, and raise you from your graves, O my people. And I will put my Spirit within you, and you shall live, and I will place you in your own

*land; then you shall know that I, the Lord, have spoken and I have
done it, says the Lord."*

Some people simply cannot keep a secret! The
moment you swear them to secrecy, they must tell it
or burst! If they manage not to tell it outright, then
they are compelled to give clues: "It's something to
eat!" — "It's something to wear." — "It's going to
happen real soon!" — "It's smaller than a breadbox."
Even nations have difficulty remaining closemouthed.
The NBC news reported Egypt, a few months ago, as
saying, "No one in Washington can keep a secret."

A mother told her son to take some homemade
butter house-to-house to sell it. "Get fifty cents a
pound for it if you can," she said, "but if you can't get
fifty cents, then take twenty-five cents." The boy went
to the first house, knocked on the door, and asked the
man if he wanted to buy some butter. "How much is
it?" the man inquired. The boy said, "Mama said to get
fifty cents if I could, but if not, to take twenty-five
cents." The man said, "Son, I'm going to teach you a
lesson. I'll take a pound of butter, and I'll pay you
twenty-five cents for it — but you must learn not to
tell everything you know. If you hadn't told me you'd
take a quarter, then I'd have been glad to give you the
half-dollar." Then he continued, "Now, do you think
you can remember that?" "Yes, sir," replied the boy,
"but I didn't tell everything I know. I didn't say nothin'
about the cat fallin' into the cream!"

God is giving clues away in this Ezekiel lesson. It is
way ahead of its time. Its author may not have had
any knowledge that there would later be a belief in an
eschatological resurrection of the dead, but many
Christian scholars believe it to be a prophecy of New
Testament Resurrection anyway. It is a powerful

picture of God's will for life for his people. It's a story of a vision given to Ezekiel.

God gave the prophet Ezekiel a vision. He was caught up in the Spirit and set down in the midst of a valley — a valley filled with dead, dry, sun-bleached, dissected bones! They were dead — you can't get any "deader" than they were! (So far, this is no "fun" vision to be involved in. It's like a nightmare that startles you wide-awake, sits you bolt upright in bed, drenched in a cold sweat and scrambling for a light to drive the "nearly-scared-to-death-feelings" away.) Then the trance continues as God asks the prophet, "Son of man, can these bones live?" Ezekiel is not about to be trapped into a wrong answer to such an impossible question, so he plays it cool and safe with a reply that has become a classic response, "O, Lord God, Thou knowest!" (How often we've said it too, "The Lord only knows!") Then the prophet is ordered to "speak to the bones." (Many a preacher has thought his lifeless flock needed just such a message as Ezekiel's word of life.) "I'm going to make you live and breathe again!" — new flesh, new muscles, new skin, new breath, new life! — and it happened just as God said and as Ezekiel prophesied!

It is now just two weeks from Easter — and God is giving more than subtle hints as to the outcome. In this text, the time is about 587 B.C. — nearly 600 years before Christ — and God is already dropping clues to the Resurrection of his Son.

The vision in the valley teaches us that —

Death Is a Fact!

You don't have to live very long to realize that literal, physical death is a fact of life. About fifty million people die each year. That figures out to 136,000 each day, 6,000 each hour, 95 each minute, and 2 each second. About twenty-five people have died while you were reading these statistics.

Death is real. We may not, today, be literally a heap of old, dry bones in a valley, but death is an apt metaphor for our "living-death" condition. The seriousness of our case is underscored by the necessity of such an extreme cure to bring us to life again. The cross points out how really dead we are. The agony of Christ's dying shows the desperate measures needed to give us life and healing.

Our situation is critical. We often don't realize if we are dead or alive. My husband, John, tells of a man who went to a wake. While he was there, he drank far too much. He got so drunk at the funeral home that the director thought he'd better not let him drive home. The undertaker put him in a casket and let him sleep it off. The next morning, when the man awoke, he said to himself, "If I'm alive, what am I doing in this casket? If I'm dead, why do I need to go to the bathroom?"

Occasionally we realize we are dead because of loss of power. We are like a child's toy that refuses to run because the batteries have been exhausted. They are "dead." Our dullness may be a result of physical weakness. Americans die of heart problems in frighteningly large numbers. It is estimated that 117,000 will be killed by cancer this year. It may be a spiritual weakness that saps our strength till we are so incapacitated, we yield to temptation, lead undisciplined lives, and barely draw a healthy breath from one day to the next.

Or maybe we are living in the dry valley of dead and broken relationships. Divorce in America is perilously close to fifty percent. Children and parents are estranged and cannot find the way back to lively rapport and harmony. Friendships lie shattered upon the dry beaches of misunderstandings and betrayals.

Then there is that fearsome valley of the uncertain future. Hope has died, dreams are shattered, and we tremblingly wonder what lies beyond death. John Baillie related how, in his last illness, a man asked his doctor what the future would be like. Just then the physician heard his dog, who had followed him to the house of his patient, scratching at the door. He told the man that his dog, of course, knew nothing of what was happening behind the door, but merely wanted to be with his master. "So," the doctor reminded the dying man, "you do not know what lies behind death's door, but you know your Master is there."

A husband and wife had worked side-by-side, preaching the Gospel of the Lord Jesus Christ as missionaries to Korea. Now, after fifteen years of labor together, she lay dying. The broken-hearted husband sat beside her bed, holding her hand and waiting for the end. She knew she meant a lot to him, and, understanding his suffering over her departure, before she closed her eyes in death, she left him this message of eternal comfort, "Do not grieve for me, my dear. You'll get me back again — you'll get me back." Just a month later, the only child of the couple fell ill and died. The father's heart was crushed a second time. He had lost his wife and now his son. But, as the boy died, he said, "Don't cry, dad. I see a light. I see mother, I see Jesus. And remember, dad, you'll get us back again." The father sat in a funeral train, escorting the body of his son to the place where he could be buried beside his mother. Two Korean women sat behind him. One of them was weeping. Her companion asked her why she was crying, and she replied, "I feel so sorry for the missionary who sits there. He lost both his wife and boy is such a short time." The other woman said, "Don't cry for him. Weep for yourself and for me. I lost a boy and I'll *never* get him back. You lost a daughter and you'll never see her again. But these foreigners who have Jesus have a strange way of getting back their dead!" — and WE DO!! Christians never see each other for the last time.

And, saddest of all deaths — we may still be dead in our sins. This was true of the nation of Israel. It is the worst death of all. Sin is so sinister and life-taking. Some months ago the newspapers and TV carried warnings about canned Alaskan salmon. If we had a 7 and ¾ ounce can of salmon, no matter what brand, we were to throw it away! If it had certain letters on the back, we could return it to the store and claim a refund, but the warning claimed that those little, harmless-looking cans of salmon might contain a deadly poison called botulism. You can't smell or taste the botulism poison, but if you eat the salmon, you will probably suffer from paralysis and likely die. It seems the poison causes people to suffocate when it paralyzes the muscles used for breathing. You can't fool around with botulism! It has to be totally and completely rejected and avoided. SIN is the same way. It is an invisible botulism that ultimately paralyzes and destroys life.

There is no doubt about it, we ARE a lot like the dead, dry bones bleaching in the valley of the vision. We are dead, and if anyone would ask if there is any hope for us, we'd have to say, "God only knows!"

But because there is more mercy in God than there is sin in us, we know that —

Dry Bones Can Live Again!

Only God can bring the dead out again, put flesh on the skeleton, cause it to stand on its feet, breathe into the body, and restore it to life.

When days are dark, God can't seem to keep from telling us there is light at the end of the tunnel. Lent is the midnight of the soul, the season of deep repentance, a time of self-examination, of beginning the Via Dolorosa pilgrimmage — but here we are, just two-thirds of the way there — and God can contain his secret no longer. We may be sinful, we may be lost, we may be a bunch of dead, dry bones, but he is going to give us life and can't keep from letting us know about it! The reason for doing it for us is simple, "My people, you shall know that I am the Lord, and have done it."

Resurrection, then, even in the midst of Lenten gloom, is not just wishful thinking. God can deal with dissected bones and lives and make them living, breathing candidates for a great, marching army!

Two women were going, by train, from one coast to the other. After dinner was over, they felt tired and decided to retire early. To save money, they were both to sleep in the same lower berth, and of course it was going to be very crowded. One of the women had barely got into bed before she decided to visit the rest room at the other end of the pullman car. When she returned, in the dark, she eased herself very carefully back into the bunk, so as not to waken her sleeping companion. The place was so small she whispered to her friend, "You know, Lil, this space is so tiny we are going to have to sleep 'spoon-fashion.'" Suddenly a hand was pressed over her mouth and a man's voice whispered in her ear, "I believe you are in the wrong berth, but you'd better not scream and draw attention to yourself. Why don't you just find your way back to your own bed without further ado?" He took his hand from her mouth, and the woman frantically rushed back to her own quarters. The next morning, at breakfast in the dining car, the "out-of-place sleeper" noticed a nice-looking man sitting across the table from her. An awful possibility flashed through her mind, "Was he the one she had crawled into bed with? Would he tell? Would he have a laugh at her expense?

Would he broadcast her mistake?" The man seemed to read her mind, steadily returned her glance, then with a broad grin and a quick wink, picked up two spoons and laid them side by side on the table!

During Lent, God's not that good at keeping a secret. This fifth Sunday in Lent is our "pre-Easter" peek at what God's raising Christ from the dead is all about. But the secret is too good. God HAD to tell someone, so he spilled the news in a vision to Ezekiel. He comes closer to telling the whole secret in the New Testament lesson of the miracle of Jesus' raising Lazarus from the dead. It's another preview of the wondrous event that is soon coming. These hurried glimpses into God's wonderful and secret plan for us are too good to keep quiet about.

Matthew's Gospel tells us that the holy family — Mary, Joseph, and Jesus — took refuge in Egypt to prevent Herod from murdering our newborn Lord. Many believe that the little family lived in the vicinity of Cairo while they were refugees. Legend has it that when the holy family stopped one time at a place on their journey, asking for food, they were told they could have it if Mary would help prepare it. In that place, according to the story, Joseph leaned on his staff and a tree started growing from the staff out of the desert sand. As evidence, the believers now point to a great, green tree which still stands there, growing and alive. Myth or not, it IS true that wherever and whenever Jesus has been permitted to take "rest," to become "rooted" in the heart of a person, he has brought life and vitality out of death. His is a "greening" which lasts through life, beyond the grave! If you are unhappy with a dull, dry, dead-bones existence, you can find new life in Christ!

If dry bones can live again, who could ever doubt that God would come to our dry valley of sin and despair and death? Soon the cool, refreshing breeze of

Easter's full return is going to come like soothing, renewing balm to your heart and soul. Christ's cross, in spite of its dreadful death, brings surging new life.

The Empress Helena one day was searching for the cross of life. Her followers searched many places and finally found three crosses in Jerusalem, but still they had to decide which of the three was Jesus' cross. They pondered a long while before somebody had an idea: They took a corpse — a dead body — and placed it on the first cross, then on the second cross, and nothing happened. But when they came to Jesus' cross, the corpse came back to life!

Why don't you look to the cross with hope? Let fear and dismay retire — Easter's life is just around the corner!

7

Bitter-Sweet Recollections

Sunday of the Passion
Isaiah 50:4-9a

"The Lord God has given Me the tongue of the learned, That I should know how to speak a word in season to him who is weary. He awakens me morning by morning, He awakens My ear to hear as the learned. The Lord God has opened My ear; and I was not rebellious, Nor did I turn away. I gave my back to those who struck Me, And My cheeks to those who plucked out the beard; I did not hide my face from shame and spitting. For the Lord God will help Me; Therefore I will not be disgraced; Therefore I have set my face like a flint, and I know that I will not be ashamed. He is near who justifies Me; who will contend with Me? Let us stand together. Who is My adversary? Let him come near Me. Surely the Lord God will help Me; Who is he who will condemn Me?"

When a loved one dies, the family and friends often gather at the home or at a funeral home, and the talk there among those standing around the casket inevitably turns to experiences with that dear, deceased loved one. Sometimes the last hours on earth are re-lived and re-told. Actions and habits of the dead are repeated, and the event of the death is described in detail again and again, and the last words are repeated over and over. It's a part of the healing process to recollect and reminisce about the one who has just died. Comfort comes from talking about it, thinking about it, and remembering. It's a bitter-sweet time: It hurts and it heals, it brings laughter and tears, and we experience personally the words of the old Gospel song which says:

"Precious mem'ries, how they linger,
How they ever flood my soul,
In the stillness of the midnight,
Precious, sacred scenes unfold."

So, lest we forget, we take time on this holy Passion Sunday to recall the memories again. We begin with this song in Isaiah. The prophets wrote better than they knew when they described the suffering servant, for we, with hindsight, find it a perfect description of Christ and what he suffered and how he reacted to the shame and torture. The words of the prophets, we claim, were perfectly fulfilled in Christ. *He* is the fulfillment of the Old Testament promises!

In our Bitter-Sweet Recollections, we recall —

The Shame of His Death (verse 7)

He was humiliated by being spit upon, right in the face. Not many things so completely register contempt for others like spitting on them, but there was Jesus, the King of Heaven, the Lord of glory, co-equal with the Father — and they hated him so much they spewed saliva in his gentle face. Their expectoration was a despicable, repulsive expression of their aversion for Christ.

His shame was further felt when he was clothed in a purple robe. With condescending contempt and cruel horse-play with reed, robe, and crown of thorns they ridiculed him as King of the Jews. But even that derogatory act was carried an ugly step further when they crucified him. Gone, then, was his own robe. The soldiers gambled for it at the foot of his cross. Gone, too, was the purple robe, and then his blessed, God-in-the-flesh body was laid bare to the shameful ignominy of the gaze of all who would witness the spectacle of his nakedness. How it must have shocked his pure and holy heart to be so ignobly exposed to all who passed by! He was deprived of all of the respectability of covering for his human form.

In our culture that nearly worships nudity, and where brevity of dress is fashionable and smart, where exposure is license for lust, we sometimes forget that for Christ, it was a vulnerability nearly unendurable. Only his desperate, divine love for us could ever have held him to the cross in naked shame. And while we are remembering it all, let's not fail to reminisce about

The Suffering He Endured (verse 6)

There was the PHYSICAL PAIN. He gave his back to the smiters. His back was lacerated with the cruel scourge (with pieces of metal tied to the end of each leather thong) until it was like a plowed field. Jewish scourging was a somewhat merciful "forty stripes save one," but the Roman cat-o-nine-tails, used on their prisoners, had no such numerical limits. They struck the victim with repeated lashes, often stopped only by the tiring of the one wielding the lash.

They pulled out his beard. Just plucking a few eyebrows is often so painful that tears sting the eye, but how about the rough jerking of his beard? It is said, "His countenance was marred more than any of the sons of men." (Isaiah 52:14)

The blessed brow wore a crown of thorns. They were poisonous and painful, and the lament of the Lenten hymn describes the agony:

"O sacred head, now wounded, With grief and
   shame weighed down,
Now scornfully surrounded With thorns, Thine
   only crown;
How pale Thou art with anguish, With sore abuse
   and scorn!
How does that visage languish Which once was
   bright as morn!"

There were the nails in his hands and feet. We can
only imagine, in our poor way, the excruciating pain
and torture of the crucifixion. It was painful and
shameful. The Greeks named the cross foolish, the
Jews called it a curse, and the Romans said it was a
disgrace. The Romans felt it was so shameful, in fact,
that only slaves, aliens, and foreigners could die on a
cross. A Roman citizen, no matter how heinous the
crime, was too good for crucifixion, yet the Son of
God died on a cross-tree! CRUCIFIED! Isn't that an
ugly word? It arouses all sorts of revulsion in us. There
are many horrible ways to die, but crucifixion has to
be among the very worst. It is ignominious, tortuous,
and shameful.

In our recalling it, we remember that when his
body was stretched prone, then nailed to the cross,
the gibbet was then picked up and dropped with a
careless thud into the rock of Golgotha's hill. Did the
flesh tear a bit more as the weight of his body found a
more secure hold around the nails?

No wonder the sun refused to shine and darkness
fell at noon. It was midnight in the middle of the day,
and the sun hid its face from the agony which lasted
from the sixth to the ninth hour of that fateful, black,
good Friday.

And don't forget the MENTAL SUFFERING. Think
how lonely he was. One of his disciples betrayed him
with a kiss. Another disciple denied him with a curse.

The others forsook him and fled. No wonder the prophet said of him: "He trod the winepress alone." (Isaiah 63:3)

And with the shame, and the physical suffering, and the mental torture, there was the awful SPIRITUAL AGONY. Forsaken by human friends, he also felt forsaken by God, crying out, "MY God, my God, why hast Thou forsaken me?" (Matthew 27:46) It is the only word of the seven from the cross that Matthew gives, and it is the only word given in the original tongue, Aramaic, "Eli, Eli, la'ma sabach-tha'-ni?"

As Jesus hung on the cross, many went by and wagged their heads. They laughed at Jesus and scornfully shook their heads, saying, "Why don't you come down from the cross? Once you could do many miracles. You saved others, save yourself!" It all seemed so ludicrous to them. It was a laughable matter.

You can tell what people are by what amuses them. How we treat sacred things, humorously or seriously, discloses something of our deepest character. They laughed at him on the cross! They laughed while they killed him. And because he still loves us, when we play the fool, it kills him!

Probably the hardest of all to bear was the weight and load of sin he carried for us all. He had never known sin, and now he bears the sin of the world! We have trouble understanding how heavy this staggering weight was to Jesus. We sin, often easily and casually, but we don't always feel it. As an Indian evangelist was preaching, a flippant youth interrupted him. "You talk about the burden of sin," he sneered. "I feel none. How heavy is the burden? Eighty pounds? Ten pounds?" The preacher answered, "Tell me, if you laid a four-hundred-pound weight on a corpse, would it feel the load?" "No, because it's dead," replied the youth. The preacher replied, "That spirit, too, is dead which feels no load of sin."

It is bitter, bitter gall as we stand around his cross, by faith re-living his time on earth with us. Maybe we say, as we do when other loved ones die, "He was so young." "He was struck down in the prime of life." "Such a shame!" "Too bad!" "I wish I could have died in his place."

William Barclay told the story of a missionary who went to an Indian village and told the story of Jesus. Then, in the evening, he showed a slide presentation of Jesus' life. When the picture of Jesus was projected against the white-washed walls of the house and the figure on the cross appeared, a man leaped up from the audience and ran to the wall, "Come down from that cross, Son of God!" he cried, "I, not you, should be hanging there!" We could all say that, "I should have died instead." But if we could have done it, it would have done the world no lasting good, for again a Lenten hymn tells us why:

"There was no other good enough, To pay the
price of sin;
He only could unlock the gate Of heav'n and let us
in."

But with the bitter — there is sweet memory too — for the Passion Week, agonizing as it was,

Had a Song! (verses 7 and 9)

True, there were sighs, groans, sweat, tears, blood, shame, agony, torture, denial, betrayal — but there was also song!

Palm Sunday rang with Hosannas: "Blessed is the King who comes in the name of the Lord! Peace in heaven and glory in the highest!" It didn't last long, but it was loud and jubilant for a time.

In the Upper Room, after the first Last Supper, they ate the bread and drank the cup and "sang a hymn." What do you suppose they sang? It was surely a Psalm, but which one? Maybe it was Psalm 95:1, "O come, let us sing to the Lord! Let us shout joyfully to the Rock of our salvation." Or perhaps it was Psalm 91:1, "He who dwells in the secret place of the Most High shall abide under the shadow of the Almighty." Or perhaps it was the reassuring words of Psalm 90:1-2, "Lord, You have been our dwelling place in all generations. Before the mountains were brought forth, or ever You had formed the earth and the world, even from everlasting to everlasting, You are God." It is possible that Jesus sang the Psalm we lean on for comfort in the dying hour, Psalm 23, "The Lord is my shepherd; I shall not want. He makes me to lie down in green pastures; He leads me beside the still waters. He restores my soul; He leads me in the paths of righteousness for His Name's sake . . ."

Even on the cross, his lamenting question, "My God, Why hast thou forsaken me?" was a song from Psalm 22.

In this song in Isaiah (vss. 7&9), we see that however much the servant suffers, nothing can tame his spirit! He sings of God's help and vindication. These stanzas show his sustained confidence in God in spite of confrontation and conflict. After all, it is his very own Father "who gives songs in the night." Dark as his travail was, one New Testament writer said, "for the *joy* that was set before Him, He endured the cross, despising the shame."

I'll See You Over There!

When you and I stand in our loss and grief, with bitter-sweet recollections of our dear ones, we whisper a parting word in the death-deaf ear, "I'll see

60

you over there," "I'll meet you in the morning." "God be with you till we meet again," — and standing at Christ's cross, we whisper today, in faith, "God be with you," — and God *was* with his Son!

In this world, truth and justice and love — ever incarnate in the wonderful Jesus of Nazareth, can be defeated and even trampled down. Trouble, despair, and death, in spite of our loving, come to us all. Romantic optimism fails us. The rope-trick of positive thinking breaks under heavy pressure. But our hope is in God's power to begin again, to renew destroyed life. We are often defeated, just as it seemed Christ was defeated on Calvary's lonely hill. But God was not conquered, and neither are we! Easter is glorious proof of God's certain victory in spite of all that the inhabitants of planet earth could do to Jesus. God vindicated his suffering servant Son and raised him from the dead — so, too, will he also raise our loved ones and us.

These are indeed Bitter-Sweet Recollections — but they are far more sweet than bitter!

8

"A" Lamb to "the" Lamb

Maundy Thursday
Exodus 12:1-14

Now the Lord spoke to Moses and Aaron in the land of Egypt, saying, "This month shall be your beginning of months; it shall be the first month of the year to you. Speak to all the congregation of Israel, saying: 'On the tenth day of this month every man shall take for himself a lamb, according to the house of his father, a lamb for a household. And if the household is too small for the lamb, let him and his neighbor next to his house take it according to the number of the persons; according to each man's need you shall make your count for the lamb. Your lamb shall be without blemish, a male of the first year. You may take it from the sheep or from the goats. Now you shall keep it until the fourteenth day of the same month. Then the whole assembly of the congregation of Israel shall kill it at twilight. And they shall take some of the blood and put it on the two doorposts and on the lintel of the houses where they eat it. Then they shall eat the flesh on that night; roasted in fire, with unleavened bread and with bitter herbs they shall eat it. Do not eat it raw, nor boiled at all with water, but roasted in fire — its head with its legs and its entrails. You shall let none of it remain until the morning, and what remains of it until morning you shall burn with fire. And thus you shall eat it: with a belt on your waist, your sandals on your feet, and your staff in your hand. So you shall eat it in haste. It is the Lord's Passover. For I will pass through the land of Egypt on that night, and will strike all the firstborn in the land of Egypt, both man and beast; and against all the gods of Egypt I will execute judgment: I am the Lord. Now the blood shall be a sign for you on the houses where you are. And when I see the blood, I will pass over you; and the plague shall not be on you to destroy you when I strike the land of Egypt. So this day shall be to you a memorial; and you shall keep it as a feast to the Lord throughout your generations. You shall keep it as a feast by an everlasting ordinance.' "

"Behold! The Lamb of God who takes away the sin of the world!"
(John 1:29b)

Today there are literally hundreds of thousands of people who have never seen a real, live lamb. To many, a lamb is an animal that a farmer raises on a quiet, peaceful farm somewhere, far from where they live in the city's din. To others, it is an animal that somehow gives up its wool for making fine, warm, winter clothing. Still others are vaguely acquainted with a lamb only in the form of the chops they purchase at the butcher's counter in the supermarket. And little children associate a lamb with the little verse that sounds good, but has no reality to them:

"Mary had a little lamb, its fleece was white as snow,
And everywhere that Mary went, the lamb was sure to go.
It followed her to school one day, This was against the rule,
It made the children laugh and play, to see a lamb at school."

(Of course, today's children, bused across town to a distant school, have not the remotest chance of having a lamb follow them there!)

The Bible tells us of two kinds of lambs: the ones with a little "l" and the Lamb with the capital "L."

The Lamb With the Little "l"

The lamb, to the Old Testament Hebrews, was terribly important. The skin of the lamb became the parchments on which they wrote the message of God. The wool of the lamb became their clothing. The meat of the lamb was food for their bodies. And it was vital, not only for their physical existence, but it was vastly important to them as they built their spiritual lives around the lamb. It became the symbol of salvation. It represented the means of their approaching God. The blood of the lamb became their sacrifice, their offering to God.

In the Old Testament, the dead sacrifices of the lamb did not take away sin, it just covered it. This is the meaning of the Day of Atonement, Yom Kippur, in Hebrew, literally the Day of Covering. The sins of the Old Testament saints were covered. Recall how God, in Eden, slew an animal, took the skins, and covered Adam and Eve so that their nakedness and shame would not show.

Before a lamb, in the Old Testament, could be properly offered to cover the people's sins, it had to meet specific qualifications. Note, in our text (Exodus 12:5), the lamb must be young (a year old), a male, and perfect (without blemish or injury).

The lamb with the little "l" kept expanding in its concept in spiritual meaning. In Abel's day, it was one lamb for one man. Abel's lamb did not atone for his brother. Cain had to have his own lamb.

Later, on the night of the Passover (Exodus 12:7), Moses had instructed the family to put the blood of a slain lamb on the doorposts and lintels of the house. When the death-angel came and saw the blood, he would pass over that house and spare them the grief of death of all the first-born (of humans and animals) there. That was one lamb for one family, for one house.

Then, as God's people journeyed from Egypt to Canaan, the Day of Atonement was instituted . It was then that the high priest gathered the entire nation together and prayed for the sins of all the people. The sins of them all, priest and people, were placed on one lamb. It was the one lamb for one nation.

The Lamb With the Capital "L"

Now we take a giant step from the Old Testament

into the New. Look! the stream is getting wider! John the Baptist announces it. Jesus comes to him in the wilderness to be baptized in the River Jordan. There, in clear, prophetic voice, John cries, "Behold! The Lamb of God, which taketh away the sin of the world." (John 1:29) John is proclaiming the Lamb for all the world! Not for one man as in Abel's day, not for one family as on Passover night, not for one nation as on the Day of Atonement, but now a LAMB FOR THE WHOLE WORLD!

Now, on this Maundy Thursday, we are sitting at the table of the Lamb of God. Jesus is lifting the bread and wine, saying, "This is my body and my blood." We Christians are building our lives around God's Lamb — the Lamb with the capital "L." The blood of Christ becomes our salvation. God's Lamb went to the cross to die for us.

Jesus, God's Lamb, is like the Old Testament sacrificial lamb in that he was young when he died, only about thirty-three years of age. He was male, he was sinless, and he was perfect.

In the Jewish home, the Passover night was never forgotten. Every year they observed the time when the death-angel had passed over and spared them. They recalled that a lamb had to die for them, just as God's Lamb had to die for us. There was no safety as long as the lamb ran around the house alive. It had to die. Blood was spilt. Peter said, "We are redeemed, not with silver and gold, but with the precious blood of a Lamb without blemish and without spot."

God's Lamb and his atoning blood goes far beyond all the blood of bulls and goats and lambs under the old covenant. Theirs only covered; ours cleanses the sins completely away!

"What can wash away my sin? Nothing but the blood of Jesus,

What can make me whole again? Nothing but the
blood of Jesus.
Oh, precious is the flow, that makes me white as
snow,
No other Fount I know, Nothing but the blood of
Jesus."

And another song says it, too:

"There is a Fountain filled with blood, drawn from
Immanuel's veins,
And sinners plunged beneath that flood, Lose all
their guilty stains."

And I grew up on a Gospel song which said,

"If you from sin are longing to be free, Look to the
Lamb of God,
He to redeem you, died on Calvary, Look to the
Lamb of God."

A man traveling through a small midwestern town
saw a beautiful church with a steeple on top. On top
of the steeple was the figure of a lamb. He inquired
why that particular symbol was there and was told the
story. When the church was being built, a worker on
the tallest part of the steeple lost his grip and fell. He
fell many feet to what seemed like certain death
below. But a man chanced to be passing by with a
herd of sheep, and the falling man happened to land
on one of the lambs. The lamb broke the man's fall
and saved his life, but the lamb died. The worker was
so grateful he climbed back on the steeple and
placed the figure of the lamb there in memory of the
animal who saved his life.

It was a Lamb which broke our fall too. Man took a
terrible fall in the Garden of Eden and has been

crippled by his sins ever since. But God's Lamb offers to give us forgiveness and salvation by his death. He died for us. He died in our place.

The true story is told of children in Vacation Church School who were studying Hebrew worship. They were five-and six-year-olds, and the teacher had them engaged in a project that would help them to visualize the lesson. She had been trying to help them to understand "sacrifice." The children had constructed a little tabernacle with a cut-away-top so you could peer down inside the entire structure (all made from a cardboard shoe box!) They even had made a little cardboard altar and colored it with crayons. It was very good, a fine replica which they had copied from pictures. As an added touch of realism, they had baked some little cookies which were cut out in the shape of lambs. Then they prepared to lay one of the little lamb cookies on the altar for a sacrifice. They were trying to choose one from the cookies which were all laid out on a sheet of waxed paper. One little fellow said, "Let's take this lamb and lay him on the altar. He's all broken and no good." And sure enough, the little lamb cookie which he selected was all cracked and ruined. No one would eat it, so they might as well be practical about it. But that's not the way with God's Lamb with the capital "L." His Lamb is sinless, spotless, pure, good, holy, perfect, without a single blemish on him. And that is the Lamb that redeems us! We may often give God our left-overs, but he gave us his best Lamb, his only Lamb!

Do Something With the Lamb

The solemn fact about this Lamb story is that the blood of the Lamb must be applied. Provision has been made for us, but it can be ignored. Cain lost out because he refused to obey and bring a lamb, the house that had no lamb's blood on Passover night was visited by death, the individual who refused the nation's offering was cast out, and the person who refuses to know God's Lamb faces death and judgment. You've got to do something about God's Lamb!

The Blood of the Lamb is applied when, by faith, we kneel at his cross. The Blood of the Lamb is applied at Baptism when God meets us in our confession. The Blood of the Lamb is applied in Holy Communion in the bread and the wine. The death-angel of judgment passes over and our sins are taken away. How glad and grateful we are that Jesus is not just any lamb among many, not "a" lamb, but "the" Lamb. No wonder we delight to pray, "Jesus, Lamb of God, have mercy on me!" In the words of the marvelous *Agnus Dei,* we plead,

> "O Christ, thou Lamb of God, that takest away the
>   sin of the world,
>   have mercy on us.
> O Christ, thou Lamb of God, that takest away the
>   sin of the world,
>   have mercy on us.
> O Christ, thou Lamb of God, that takest away the
>   sin of the world,
>   grant us thy peace. Amen."

9

What Do You See?

Good Friday
Isaiah 52:13-53:12

Behold, My Servant shall deal prudently, He shall be exalted and extolled and be very high. Just as many were astonished at you, so His visage was marred more than any man. And His form more than the sons of men; So shall He sprinkle many nations. Kings shall shut their mouths at Him; For what had not been told them they shall see, And what they had not heard they shall consider.

Who has believed our report? And to whom has the arm of the Lord been revealed? For He shall grow up before Him as a tender plant, And as a root out of dry ground. He has no form or comeliness; and when we see Him, there is no beauty that we should desire Him. He is despised and rejected by men, a man of sorrows, and acquainted with grief. And we hid, as it were, our faces from Him; He was despised, and we did not esteem Him.

Surely He has borne our griefs and carried our sorrows; yet we esteemed Him stricken, smitten by God, and afflicted. But He was wounded for our transgressions, He was bruised for our iniquities; the chastisement of our peace was upon Him, and by His stripes we are healed. All we like sheep have gone astray; we have turned, every one, to his own way; and the Lord has laid on Him the iniquity of us all.

He was oppressed and He was afflicted, yet He opened not His mouth; He was led as a lamb to the slaughter. And as a sheep before its shearers is dumb, so He opened not his mouth. He was taken from prison and from judgment, and who will declare His generation? For He was cut off from the land of the living; for the transgressions of my People He was stricken. And they made His grave with the wicked — But with the rich at His death, because He had done no violence, nor was any deceit in His mouth.

Yet it pleased the Lord to bruise Him; He has put Him to grief. When You made His soul an offering for sin, He shall see His seed,

He shall prolong His days, and the pleasure of the Lord shall prosper in His hand. He shall see the travail of His soul, and be satisfied. By His knowledge my righteous Servant shall justify many, for He shall bear their iniquities. Therefore I will divide Him a portion with the great, and He shall divide the spoil with the strong, because He poured out His soul unto death, and He was numbered with the transgressors, and He bore the sin of many, and made intercession for the transgressors."

Good Friday is the Day of the Cross. Christians make a lot of the cross of Christ. I carry a cross in my change purse. I have a cross on a charm bracelet. My John carries a cross in his pocket. I wear a cross necklace at all times that my John gave me. I have a cross of crystal on my piano that my daughter, Jodi gave us. John has a wooden cross over his study desk. We have, in our home, a large, wooden, hand-carved, lovely cross that came from Oberammergau. It is a three-foot cross with the suffering Savior hanging on it.

There is a cross on the altar in most churches, and many a church has a cross crowning its steeple.

We Christians sing hymns of the cross: "In the Cross of Christ I Glory," "The Old Rugged Cross," "When I Survey the Wondrous Cross," "Beneath the Cross of Jesus," "Jesus, Keep Me Near the Cross," and many, many others.

The cross is a symbol of the Christian faith. The tool of torture becomes the pride of our profession. It's strange, when you stop to think about it. Imagine someone holding up a rope, a hangman's noose, and saying, "This is a sign of my faith." Or think of wearing a small, intricate, electric chair on a gold chain and calling it "a symbol of faith." Yet, an execution-beam, a cross, is the sign of the Christian faith, and we wear and display it proudly.

Crosses have been a symbol of shame for years. Only the vilest and meanest of criminals were given this ugly death. Some of the worst men of history have died on a cross: killers, thieves, robbers, renegades — these have stained the ugly beams of the cross with human blood.

Suppose we read the text again. Actually, the cross is not even mentioned in these verses. Yet, who can thoughtfully read them without a lonely hill outside the city walls of Jerusalem coming to mind? It is virtually impossible for Christians to read this fourth of the Servant songs without thinking of Jesus.

Scholars and Bible readers keep asking the question: "Who is this Suffering Servant?" Some have said it is the nation of Israel, others suggest it is the prophet himself, some say it is an early martyr, and still others believe it is the expected Messiah. No matter, it still applies sweetly and accurately to the Passion of Jesus. I, personally, simply cannot read these words in Isaiah 52 and 53 without feeling a certainty that it is a nearly perfect picture of our dying Savior.

Look at these words again. What do you see?

See a Spectacle of Suffering

Humanity has a fascination with the gory, the ugly, and the dying. We are eager for the spectacular. We go to airshows and thrill at the maneuvers of the wing-walker, the "delayed" parachute opening, the "close-to-the-earth-spin," and gasp and wonder if the pilot can pull the plane out in time.

Or we go see a rodeo. Men on nearly wild, bucking horses are propelled out of chutes, and we ask ourselves how many seconds the rider will stay on and how high he will be thrown, and how many bones will break when he lands?

Evel Knievel rode his SkyCycle in a leap of death

as he tried to jump the Snake River Canyon, and spectators paid twenty-five dollars each for the thrill of a few seconds.

At the Indianapolis 500 a car misses a curve, crashes into a wall, bursts into flames, and we enjoy another breath-taking thrill.

A matador faces a bull in Mexico City, the bull is defeated or the matador is gored to death, and a raucous crowd shouts, "Ole! Ole! Ole!"

We go to see movies that depict suffering, fear, violence, gore, and blood. On television we watch an average of six acts of violence each hour.

We humans have not really changed too much since Jesus' day. We still massacre each other in wars, kill each other on the highways, murder about fifty people a day in America, and rape someone every twelve seconds.

So the cross is just another wide-screen spectacular that captivates us. The picture of the Suffering Servant, despised and rejected of men, Man of sorrows, acquainted with grief, visage marred, scourged, smitten, oppressed, afflicted, bruised, forsaken — to many, he is just another thrill to behold the torture that a human can endure when dying. That gibbet of shame, holding the thorn-crowned head and nail-riven body is only a Suffering Spectacular. Some can behold him without feelings of pity, regret, grief, or remorse.

On the other hand, some compassionate, tender-hearted souls identify with the pain until that's *all* they see. A hair-dresser told me recently, "I don't like the sadness of Lent. Songs and portrayals of the cross depress me. I prefer the joy and celebration of Easter! Why can't we just by-pass all the bad stuff?"

Still others . . .

See Sin and Feel Hatred and Guilt
That Caused the Suffering

We read, "He was bruised for our iniquities; the chastisement of our peace was upon Him, and by His stripes we are healed. All we like sheep have gone astray; we have turned every one to his own way; and the Lord has laid on Him the iniquity of us all." and "You made His soul an offering for sin." and then a feeling of guilt possesses some of us.

We may feel an individual guilt, we may admit to corporate sin, but in any event, we have to admit, "He didn't sin, I   did, he was pure, but I am impure; he was holy, but I am unholy."

Seeing and watching the holy, sinless, perfect Son of God die in such torture for my sins makes me feel terrible, overwhelming guilt. The feeling is somewhat like the vain regret we feel for our thoughtless actions toward a loved one who has died. A wife said of her recently deceased husband, "He always wanted a canary, but I didn't want the bother of having it in the house. I wish now I had given him what he asked for. I had a bird carved on his headstone, at the cemetery, but I think it was too late to do much good."

So, we see Christ dying for our sins, and say, regretfully, "I wish I had not done it. I wish I were not so sinful and impure," and the guilt of our sinning hangs heavily upon us.

Once we get a clear picture of Jesus bearing our sins on the tree (I mean your sins and mine actually nailing him to the cross), then we shall never be able to sin easily and comfortably again. If the exceeding sinfulness of sin ever fully dawns upon us, we'll know it is a crucifying thing. It was not the Jews, nor the Roman soldiers, but sin that nailed Christ to the cross!

Consider this as an example: I've always hated cancer. I hated it when I first knew what kind of loathsome disease it was when it fastened itself upon the human body. I hated it even more when I became a pastor and visited my people in hospitals and saw persons suffering and struggling with its hold upon them. But I'll tell you when I hated cancer most. It was when I stood by a bedside in Mexico, Missouri, and saw a gracious, saintly woman suffering agony and torment, gasping for her next breath. That dying woman was my mother, and from that day to this, I find cancer abhorrent, loathsome, and despicable, and I rejoice in every victory that medicine makes over it!

So it is with sin. I hate it when I see what it does to our world. It causes war and greed and makes us kill one another. It makes people ugly, proud, mean, selfish, and causes them to act like the devil. It makes me mean, thoughtless, and unkind. But I hate sin most when I look at the cross and see there the fairest face that ever was, turned into a bloody thing. I see our sins stabbing him, tearing him, and finally killing him — and then I despise sin with a passion. No wonder Martin Luther cried out, "O my sins! my sins!" — and we echo, "Mine too, mine too!"

See Love in the Suffering Servant

Above and beyond everything, in the suffering servant, we see LOVE! Unfathomable, indescribable, unbelievable, unending, undying love illuminates the Savior. This love is represented by the horizontal cross-arm of the cross on which he died. Love that reaches how far? Mark Spitz, the Olympic swimmer who won seven gold medals for the United States, says that in training for the games he swam the distance of twice around the world's equator, about 50,000 miles! Incredible, isn't it? But God's love stretches wider and broader and farther than that. It is love that reaches every nation, every tribe, every tongue, every color, everybody!

The other dimension of Christ's love is represented by the vertical arm of the cross. It is the love that stretches all the way from heaven to earth. How deep does it go? Sometime ago it was found that the deepest point in the Atlantic Ocean was off Puerto Rico, a depth of 30,236 feet. In 1893, a Norwegian explorer, Nanssey, was attempting to plumb the depths of the Artic Ocean. He came to a point where all the rope was let down and still the bottom was not reached. He wrote in his log book, "Deeper than that!" The Atlantic may be more than 30,000 feet deep, but God's love is "deeper than that!" It is as deep as the worst sinner, deeper than Mary Magdalene's seven-demon-possession, deeper than Judas' betrayal, deeper than Peter's denial, deeper than your most deeply hidden sin. Charles Wesley wrote so movingly:

"O Love divine, what hast Thou done!
    Th' incarnate God hath died for me!
The Father's co-eternal Son
    Bore all my sins upon the tree!
The Son of God for me hath died:
    My Lord, my Love, is crucified."

What Do "You" See?

If you are only a spectator, the gory scene will soon be forgotten. Lent is soon over and you can think of chocolate-covered, marshmallow Easter bunnies, colored eggs, and what new clothes you will wear this spring. But, if you have felt guilt for sin and then see his matchless love, then you will want to respond to him in passionate commitment and loyalty. Count Zinzendorf was a royal prince, a prodigal, licentious playboy who loved high living. Then one day he saw a huge painting of the suffering, crucified Savior. Beneath the painting were these words, "All this I have done for thee, what hast thou done for Me?" His heart was touched, his life was changed, and he became the leader of the Moravians. He came to America and was the spiritual Father of the Moravian Church. It all came from the cross — and his gratitude was expressed in commitment which lasted for life.

Whether or not you enjoy Easter's triumph depends largely on what you see in the cross of God's Suffering Servant, but you can live in Easter's triumph if you die a little in Calvary's crucifixion.

Why No Old Testament Lessons For Easter?

There are no Old Testament lections for the Easter season in Series A because the Old Testament does not know anything about the Resurrection. The best it can do for us is translation: as in Enoch and Elijah.

Even the doctrine of immortality was a late development and only came into prominence in the time of Second Isaiah. Job's question, "If a man die, shall he live again?" was not fully answered until Christ and the New Testament. Death, in the Old Testament, was just a prison house, a dark dungeon, without light and hope.

Logically, then, the ones who chose the lections for the Easter season have taken Lesson I for each Sunday from the Book of Acts, with two exceptions — Easter Sunday, Series B, is Isaiah 25:6-9 and Easter Sunday, Series C, is Exodus 15:1-11.

10

Death Is Damned!

Easter
Acts 10:34-43

"And we are witnesses of all things which He did both in the land of the Jews and in Jerusalem, whom they killed by hanging on a tree. Him God raised up on the third day, and showed Him openly."

In a secular society, Easter cannot even begin to compete with Christmas! But we try . . .

Sometimes even Christians are ignorant of the facts of Easter. In Clearwater, Florida, a man and his wife took us out to dinner during a revival. They told the legendary story of a Roman Catholic who appeared at the Pearly Gates and asked St. Peter for entrance. St. Peter said, "All right, tell me, what is Easter?" The Catholic said, "Oh, that's the day that some fellow discovered America, isn't it?" "No, that's wrong, and you'll have to go below," said Peter. Next came a United Methodist, asking to enter heaven. St. Peter asked him, "What's Easter?" The United Methodist replied, "Oh, that's the day that big, fat, jolly man with a big bag of toys comes around." "No, you're wrong," said Peter. "You can't come inside." Then a Lutheran came and he *almost* made it. He wanted to get into heaven also, and when Peter asked him, "What's Easter?" he said, "Easter? Isn't that the story about the man who died, was buried, and on the third day, came alive, rolled the stone from his grave, looked out and saw his shadow, then went back inside for six more weeks of winter?"

Most of you have better knowledge of the biblical truth than this poor story, but many people in our world do not. But with or without the truth, the world has still jumped on the Christian Easter Bandwagon and become a part of the Easter act with spending. In America, in 1980, we spent ninety million dollars on Easter cards, 550 million dollars on Easter candy, one billion dollars on Easter clothes, and an undisclosed amount on Easter toys and the Easter bunny.

I'm not against the Easter bunny (so don't get up-tight this early in the sermon), but you have to admit it would take a non-spiritual world to dream up a rabbit to replace resurrection, wouldn't it? A rabbit that lays eggs, at that! Come to think of it, if we can make our modern, no-longer-innocent-of-the-facts-of-life-kids believe *that* story, surely they'll have no problem at all with the empty tomb!

Humanity's Worst!

"*They* killed by hanging on a tree." (v. 39)

We Christians have just gone through the six weeks of preparation, repentance, confession, and journeying toward the cross of Good Friday. We read this text and realize the "they" who killed Jesus is "us."

We've understood afresh that the shed blood of Christ, his sacrificial death was God's way of spanning the chasm between a holy God and sinful humans. The shedding of the blood of Jesus was a necessary price for our redemption from sin's destruction. God cannot look lightly upon sin and therefore cannot forgive sin lightly. He is holy and looks upon sin with deadly seriousness. We may treat it casually, but he does not. For all his abounding, amazing, limitless love, he is also the sovereign Judge of the Universe and has uncompromising standards for its moral order. Christ's death and his shed blood for us is God's solution for our problem. He loves us infinitely and is willing to pay at measureless cost to himself for our freedom — still upholding his own holiness and righteous rule over the universe.

Christ's death was God's divine effort to secure our salvation and be free to accept us. This is the wondrous paradox that we have considered throughout Lent. Perhaps just as paradoxical, God allowed it to be brought about by those wicked ones he wanted to save. The unholy killed the holy so the sinless could bring life to the sinful. Before Christ came, men went to the cross to die, but since HE died, we look to the cross to live!

That was the worst we sinful humans could do . . . and it was BAD!

"*Him* God raised up on the third day." (vs. 40)

Easter says, "You can put Truth in a grave, but it won't stay there!" Here is the keystone of our faith: *GOD RAISED JESUS FROM THE DEAD!* Christianity stands or falls upon the FACT of the RESURRECTION OF CHRIST! It is not one of the many bricks in the masonry of Christianity; it is the cornerstone, the foundation upon which the whole edifice rests. We do not give our loyalty and allegiance to a still-dead Leader.

Buddha died, and he is still dead.
Confucious died, and he is still dead.
Mohammed died, and he is still dead.
Joseph Smith died, and he is still dead.
Jesus Christ died, and HE ROSE AGAIN!

Christianity is the only religion whose leader died and

rose again. We are not giving our lives to a dead corpse.

As Easter approached, a Sunday School teacher had a project to teach the meaning of Easter to the children. She collected a number of egg-shaped boxes used by Leggs pantyhose and gave one to each child, asking them to find one thing that reminded them of Easter and to place it in the egg-box. On Easter Sunday, the children brought their boxes to the teacher, who opened them one by one. The first child had a rock in his egg; it was to represent the door of the tomb. Another child had a flower to speak of new life. A third had a butterfly, also representing life. The fourth child had nothing in his egg, for, he explained, "The tomb of Jesus was EMPTY!"

And that's a glorious truth! The blessed body is no longer lying in Joseph's new tomb. Have you ever stopped to think of the wonder that Joseph of Arimathea must have felt? He is, on Easter morning, now the possessor of one slightly used tomb. How many people do you know with an experience as unique as that? When you use a grave, you expect to use it forever, but Joseph's new tomb is used by his Master for only three days and nights. Ever after, to Joseph, it must have had the fragrance of Resurrection life in it. No stinking, mouldering grave for Joseph; now he owns one that is aromatic with the fragrance of life and hope and triumph beyond death and the grave! Notice the sweet aroma of the Easter lilies this morning: Joseph's tomb must have smelled like that.

Christ's resurrection means we live now, never to die again. Oh, sure, our bodies may wither and die, yes, but "we" live on forever! Danny Thomas tells the story of his father's last illness. His father realized he was very near to the end of his life. One thing he wanted, above all else, was that all his family should be with him at this time. They all responded to his call.

He had a visit with each of them, and then asked them to all gather together near his bedside. He looked around at those who were dearest to him. Then Danny Thomas saw his father turn his face to the wall and heard him whisper a prayer in the words, "God damn death!" Don't get hung up on his use of the four-letter word but think about it. In the providence of God, Easter comes again as if in response to that prayer. For in the cross, the burial, the stone that was rolled away, the empty tomb, and the resurrection of Jesus Christ, isn't this exactly what God has done? "Death is swallowed up in victory!" It is this dimension of eternity that makes life meaningful now. It is the assurance that our labors for justice and mercy and love are not in vain. No wonder Easter calls forth the Hallelujahs. God really has damned death!

And in damning death, God has emptied death of its power over us. One December day in Edinburgh, in 1666, Hugh Mackail, "the youngest and bravest of the covenanting ministers," was brought before his judges. They condemned him to death on the scaffold. He had just four days in which to live. The soldiers led him back to Tolbooth prison. Hosts of people gathered to see him. Many wept as the young minister passed by them. But no one saw any tears in his eyes. There was not the least trace of self-pity. This Sir Galahad of the Cross, as James Stewart calls him, showed only a shining, radiant, face. Catching a glimpse of a friend in the crowd, he shouted, "Good news, good news! I am within four days' journey of enjoying the sight of Jesus Christ!"

God's best, done for us on Easter, lets us face life or death or whatever, like that.

Death Is Damned!

So go ahead and enjoy Easter in our secular world.

But be aware it is all short-lived. The greeting cards will be read and tossed away, the new clothes will soil and wear out, the chocolate-covered-marshmallow Easter bunny will make you fat if you eat it (and melt if you don't). The colored candy eggs (if you're lucky) are soon gone, and even the lovely Easter lilies will fade and wilt and die — but Christ, conqueror of death, hell, and the grave, is alive forevermore!

God has taken the cross of his Son and used it as a battering ram to knock the ends out of the grave and let in the light of the dawning of a new day! A young Christian in the early church stood before a Roman magistrate, who said, "I sentence you to death for your faith in Jesus Christ, the Nazarene!" The man staunchly replied, "Sir! Death is dead! So you cannot frighten me!"

Danny Thomas' father, for all his rough, crude language, was more right than he knew. Death *is* damned! Alleluia! Alleluia!

No Longer Spectators —
But Participants!

Second Sunday of Easter
Acts 2:14a, 22-32

But Peter, standing up with the eleven, raised his voice and said to them, "Men of Israel, hear these words: Jesus of Nazareth, a man attested by God to you by miracles, wonders, and signs which God did through Him in your midst, as you yourselves also know —

Him being delivered by the determined counsel and foreknowledge of God, you have taken by lawless hands, have crucified, and put to death;

whom God raised up, having loosed the pains of death, because it was not possible that He should be held by it.

This Jesus God has raised up, of which we are all witnesses."

Last Sunday was a High Day — the loftiest of them all — Resurrection Day! Easter-lily fragrance filled the church, choirs sang their gladdest anthems of triumph; worshipers, wearing fresh, maybe even new, spring outfits, participated in the service with unusual fervor and expectancy; even delinquent members, who seldom show up for church, arranged for their annual pilgrimage to be part of the joyous day.

But today, attendance is down (to normal or below), the lilies are gone, the choir has packed "Christ the Lord Is Risen Today" away for another year, and we are back to the "business-as-usual," everyday-routine of worship. The "After-Easter-Letdown" has struck again! Own it, face it, confront it, admit it, and then get your perspectives back in order.

This calls for a review of what we've been about this past six weeks of Lenten preparation and last Sunday's Easter celebration. Peter, in the text, stands up and recapitulates the story of Jesus to the multitude in Jerusalem. He proclaimed all that God had done in Christ. Peter proclaimed to the spectators, and now we are participants in the message.

Peter Told How God Had Publicly Endorsed Jesus

God gave aid to his Son, Jesus, by doing mighty miracles through him. (Acts 2:22!) That is pretty strong endorsement when God aids his Son by doing miracles like turning water into wine, healing the sick, exorcising demons, and even controlling nature (as when he calmed the storm at sea).

It was no less favorable acknowledgement when God fulfilled his own divine, pre-arranged plan for his Son by letting the Roman government nail him to a cross and murder him. (vs. 23) The cross was no accident. Over and over again we are reminded that the cross is in the eternal plan of God. We must never set God and Jesus against one another, making God heavy, angry, and wrathful, and Jesus sweet, gentle, and loving. It was by God that Jesus came! But still, God allowed wicked humanity to kill him. The crucifixion was the greatest crime in history. It shows what sin will do. Sin took the purest life and fairest form that ever lived in this dark world and nailed it to a cross.

And the final, grand stamp of God's favor was placed on his Son when he brought him back to life again. (vs.24) Three days, God felt, were long enough to prove his point, and he raised Jesus from the dead! The ugly tyrant of death lost its grip on Jesus. It simply couldn't get a good hold on him.

Did you ever try to hold onto a greased pig or a raw egg white? It will slither right out of your grasp no matter how much you try to confine it. Death was even more helpless than that when God said, "Enough!" and gave his Son a glorious, unheard of, never-to-be-repeated-by-any-imposter   Resurrection! We must never limit this grand truth to one Sunday in the year. Every Sunday is the Lord's Day and every Lord's Day is an anniversary of the Resurrection.

When we only observe this event, when we take the place of spectators, it leaves us often with nothing to say. Kurt Vonnegut, contemporary novelist, tells of a meeting which occurred between two novelists, Nelson Algren and Jose' Donoso. Vonnegut introduced them as they were coming up a stairway and, in the process, told Algren that Donoso was from Chile. Algren shook Donoso's hand, but couldn't think of anything to say to the Chilean novelist. Finally, after a long, uncomfortable silence between the two strangers, Algren said, "It must be nice to come from a country that's so long and narrow."

We can talk of by-gone miracles, we can be avid watchers at the foot of Golgotha's gory, gruesome gibbet, we can remain awe-struck beholders of the .empty grave — but when we have *experienced* the miracle of forgiveness, when our sins are laid on the shoulders of Calvary's victim, when we have been raised to walk in newness of life — suddenly we are participants in the divine drama of the ages, and become flaming zealots as we witness to the event!

We Are Witnesses (Participants) in the Resurrection
(verse 32)

We now get to be involved in Christ's life, be a part of it, and tell everybody what God has done!

We Can Tell Every Doubter That We
Meet of Christ's Life

When we see those who, like the Emmaus Road disciples, are sad and despondent, having lost their faith in all they once held as high hope, we can say, "Don't worry about it. It was part of the divine plan that Christ should die. He ought to have suffered. The prophets foretold it. But that dark day is now past, and Jesus is truly alive!"

We can tell them how our own hearts have been strangely warmed as the same winsome Stranger of the Emmaus Road now stops in our homes too and transforms them into places of communion with the risen Lord. We can reassure the doubters that, at their invitation, he will also walk and eat and stay with them. F.H. Lyte expressed it in the words of his famous hymn:

"Abide with me: fast falls the eventide,
The darkness deepens; Lord with me abide!
When other helpers fail, and comforts flee,
Help of the helpless, Oh, abide with me!"

We can also witness to those doubters like Thomas who, in the Gospel lesson, thought the resurrection of Jesus was just too good to be true. Haven't nearly all of us felt like Thomas? He had been ready to die with Jesus at the time of Lazarus' death. He doubted, he had no faith, he had no hope, and yet, after the crucifixion, he hung around a little longer just because he loved him. While Thomas was doubting the resurrection, Jesus came through locked doors, saying, "Peace be with you." He included the dear doubter in his salutation of peace.

We can witness to all who doubt that Jesus was not put-out with Thomas for his questionings. Instead, Jesus lets Thomas know how fully he understands. How good Christ always is: he knows about our doubts of him, but he does not doubt us in return. Jesus stoops down to where the doubter is — downward — that's always the direction that God works. Down from heaven to earth, down from Creator to Savior, down from glory to shame, down from the divine to become a man. In his encounter with Thomas, Jesus lowers himself again, going right down into the soul of the man that cannot believe!

We've been there too, haven't we? We are witnesses to our own feeble, frail faith, our fierce fears and our damaging, damning doubts. But he came down to us, too, and shored up our reeling faith with a word of "Peace be with you."

Maybe we all know people who haven't the foggiest idea of what orthodox Christianity is all about. Will we lecture them on what they "ought" to do, shame them for their poor theology, embarrass them for their "no faith," or will we, like Jesus, stoop and be witnesses to what it is like when Jesus comes into our life? Witnessing thus to the doubters conquers the unbelief. Faith comes to Thomas, and he responds, "My Lord and my God!"

There are side benefits to this kind of participation. Our own faith is bolstered, and we are left with new confidence for ourselves. John McKay of the NFL tells a story illustrating the supreme confidence of Bear Bryant, University of Alabama football coach. McKay and Bryant had been out shooting ducks for about three hours, and after a while, one lonely duck flew by. The Bear fired, and that duck is still flying today. But as Bear watched the duck flap out of sight, he looked at McKay and said, "John, you are witnessing a real miracle. There flies a dead duck!"

So, all of us are witnesses to the Lord who has bent to our skepticism and made believers of us anyway. He did not argue with us but won us as he took us by the hand. So now, as participating disciples, we try, not to "prove" anyone into faith, not to force, not to argue, not to shame — we just attempt to show the doubters a bit of the glory we have seen. We may never astound them with our long, involved dissertations on creeds, but we have had a part in the resurrection, and we simply invite them to meet the Master who can give them life and his peace.

We Can Tell Every Sinner of the Resurrection Life They Can Have

Along life's road there are not only doubters but the sinful. They are like Mary Magdalene, literally dying to know they can be free. She had not only not been good, she had been possessed by seven devils, but Christ's forging love cast them out and set her free.

Devils in our lives come by different names, but our risen Christ has conquered death, hell, and the grave, and he is not stymied by the strong demons that ensnare our soul and enslave our lives. As rescued, redeemed, resurrected, forgiven disciples, we get to tell others how that came about.

Remember that our witness to the failing, fallen sinful (in and out of the church) is one of loving concern. A woman in Florida told of occasionally visiting a certain church. One morning she was sick and therefore could not attend. She reported that twelve different people from the church came that afternoon to her home to see about her and to assure her of their concern. Since we've all been there sometime in our lives, we need to let the sick, hurting, and sinful know we are caring for them. Sinners must always be made welcome in the church (or at least they *should* be). A man in a Georgia town where Miller beer is made reported seeing this sign in a certain church: "Miller people not welcome here!" Jesus would *never* say that! The church should never say it. We are witnesses, as was Mary Magdalene, to the fact that we once were possessed by devils we could not rid ourselves of. Sometimes we let circumstances enslave us; other times, it was things that we did that ensnared us; sometimes our weak wills kept us from doing what was right — we've struggled with nearly every known sin in the book and were losing the battle until the mighty, risen Christ burst our bonds and set us free!

In a textile factory where threads are made into fabric, there is a sign above the machines which reads, "If the threads become tangled, call the foreman." A new employee found the threads on her machine badly tangled. Frantically she tried to untangle them. The foreman came by and said, "Why didn't you call for me?" She replied, "I was just trying to do my best by myself." He chided her, saying, "Doing your best includes calling the foreman." Some things we cannot do for ourselves. We cannot stop sinning on our own. We cannot save ourselves. We cannot make ourselves good, but we are witnesses to the incredible truth that the risen Lord will straighten out our lives for us!

A little boy was visiting his grandparents. He was given his first sling. He had fun playing with it in the woods. He would take aim, let the stone fly, and wait for it to hit the target. But he never hit a thing. Then, on his way home for dinner, he cut through the backyard and saw Grandmother's pet duck. He took aim and let the stone fly. It went straight to the mark and the duck fell dead. The little boy panicked. In frightened desperation, he took the dead duck and hid it in the woodpile. Then he saw his sister, Sally, standing over by the corner of the house. She had seen the whole thing. They went in to dinner. Sally said nothing. After dinner, Grandmother said, "O.K., Sally, let's clear the table and wash the dishes." Sally said, "Oh, Grandmother, Johnny said he wanted to help you in the kitchen today. Didn't you, Johnny?" Then she leaned over and whispered to him, "Remember the duck." So Johnny did the dishes. Later in the day, Grandfather called the children to go fishing. Grandmother said, "I'm sorry, but Sally can't go. She has to stay here and help me clean the house and get supper." Sally smiled, "That's all been taken care of. Johnny said he wanted to help you today, didn't you, Johnny?" Then she whispered, "Remember the duck." This sort of thing went on for several days. Johnny did all the chores, his and those assigned to Sally. Finally, he could stand it no longer, so he went to his Grandmother and confessed it all. His Grandmother took him in her arms and said, "I know, Johnny. I was standing at the kitchen window and saw the whole thing. And because I love you, I forgave you. And knowing that I loved you and would always forgive you, I wondered just how long you would let Sally make a slave of you."

As witnesses to the freedom from sin's slavery that the risen Christ gives us, we proclaim liberation to every captive of the devil that we meet. Oswald Chambers said, "You can never give another what you have found, but you can make him homesick for what you have!"

He Rose Again!

A man stood in front of the window of an art store

in which a picture of the crucifixion of our Lord was on display. He was gazing intently at the display; the bleeding, dying, suffering form of the man on the middle cross had captured all his thoughts, and he was barely conscious of another person who stood beside him. Finally, turning around, he noticed a little boy with his eyes, too, fixed upon the scene. He was just a ragged little mite of humanity, standing there in torn clothes. The man thought he would see if the boy knew what the picture was about, so he said, "Son, do you know who that is?" The child was quick to reply, "Yes, sir," pointing to the man on the middle cross, "That's our Savior." He was so surprised that that the man seemed not to know about him, and with a bit of pity in his voice, the boy eagerly told him the story of Jesus. "So," he continued, "them's the soldiers," pointing to the Romans who had nailed Christ to the cross. Then, pointing to a woman near the edge of the crowd, he said, "That's his mother, see. The woman who is crying." He pushed his hands deep into his pockets, as if waiting to see if the man wanted another answer about the scene. After a long silence, the boy said, "Yes, sir, that's Jesus, and they killed him." "Where did you learn all this?" the man asked. "At Sunday School, sir," the boy replied. The man, with mingled feelings, turned once again to the crucifixion scene in the window and after a moment slowly walked away. The little street urchin was left looking at the picture alone. The man had not walked more than two blocks when he heard the sound of small feet beating exultantly on the sidewalk and a childish voice crying, "Mister! say, Mister!" Turning around, the man saw the same little lad running toward him. He was nearly out of breath, but when he reached him, he cried out triumphantly and joyously, "I forgot to tell you, "HE ROSE AGAIN! Yes, Mister, HE ROSE AGAIN! That's the most important part!"

It *is* the most important part. We have no need for "After-Easter-Letdown." We are now made not just spectators, but participants, joyful witnesses to a sick, doubting, sinful, dying world, that because he lives, we live — and they can live also!

12
Are There Two Baptisms?

Third Sunday of Easter
Acts 2:14a, 36-47

*Then Peter said to them, "Repent, and let every one of you be
baptized in the name of Jesus Christ for remission of sins; and you
shall receive the gift of the Holy Spirit."*

Misinformation is often passed around as Gospel
truth. It is like the two little boys who were talking
between themselves. One of them couldn't understand
why they had holes in their tummies — where did their
belly-buttons come from? But his little five-year-old
friend had a ready answer. "Oh, that's easy," he said.
"You see, God makes us all up in heaven and then
sends us down to earth, but before we can come down
to earth, we have to pass inspection. So God lines us all
up in a row and goes down the line, and when we are
all ready to leave for earth, he pokes each one of us in
the tummy and says, 'You're done, you're done, you're
done!'" Now any mother will tell you, it really doesn't
happen that way, but still the child passed out his
misunderstanding as truth.

Times without number I've been asked (and
maybe you have, too), "Have you been baptized in the
Holy Spirit?" If I say, "Yes," the subject is closed, the
interrogator is happy and satisfied. But if I say, "I've

been baptized in water," immediately I come under a barrage of further questions like, "But have you spoken in tongues?" or "Have you had a 'special' experience?" or "Do you have a true baptism and infilling of the Spirit?" Then the questioner will often continue, "You know there are two baptisms, don't you; Water Baptism and Spirit Baptism?"

This is the misinformation of a lot of people who have not had proper instruction in this matter.

The Holy Spirit Comes at Your Baptism

The text says, "Repent, and be baptized in the name of Jesus Christ for the remission of sins; and you shall RECEIVE THE GIFT OF THE HOLY SPIRIT."

Paul describes baptism as a dying and being buried with Christ, so that in baptism, the old, sinful self dies, and, in Christ, we rise again in the newness of life. Baptism is really a resurrection experience.

Helmut Thielicke, the famous German preacher, tells of a story he heard in South Africa. A group of primitive bushmen from the backwoods were taken to a modern, technical exhibition which included the marvelous developments of civilization. They could neither write nor read and had never been out of the brush. Now they were whisked for a ride in a jet plane and given the full treatment of modern technology. Everyone wondered what would impress these stone-age natives most. The scientists were sure it would be either the flight at 35,000 feet at some 550 miles per hour or the electronic brain. It was neither. These bushmen were most fascinated by an ordinary kitchen water faucet. To them, it was an absolute, unparalleled miracle! Water, for them, was often hard to get, sometimes impossible, and always difficult to carry. Now, precious water was made to flow out of a wall before their very eyes. The flight in the sky by jet and the marvelous computer were something out of a fairyland to them. But water out of a wall related to everyday life. They knew thirst, they knew drought, and here was something that met them at their point of need. This is what the Holy Spirit does for us in baptism. He brings God near. He is no longer a God afar off but close at hand, when and where we need him!

Without the Holy Spirit's coming to us at baptism, we could not know Christ as our Savior. Jesus told us that everyone who enters the Kingdom must be born of the Spirit. The Holy Spirit comes to us at our baptism, and in the words of the Baptismal formula, causes us to be born anew.

It is the work of the Holy Spirit to create faith in Christ. This is the witness of the Apostle Paul who said, "No man can say Jesus is Lord except by the spirit." This is sometimes difficult to believe. It is "too good to be true!" After all, how can one man, by his death on an ugly cross, do away with *my* sins? That man died hundreds of years ago — others have died on crosses before and since — how is *his* death any different? We simply could not handle it with rational thinking unless faith were given us by the Holy Spirit. He implants the faith in our hearts. He helps us see Jesus Christ as the Son of God, the Savior of the world. He is ever the Agent of our conversion.

We cannot earn the Spirit, we cannot work ourselves into a high emotional pitch to receive him, we can't buy him (Simon the Sorcerer once tried that and was soundly rebuked by the disciples).

The Spirit comes normally through the channel of the Word of God. He comes to us in the Word and Sacraments. Paul said, "Take the Sword of the Spirit, which is the Word of God." Word and Spirit are inseparable. When Jesus was baptized of John in the River Jordan, the Holy Spirit came upon him. When you were baptized, he came to you in response to your faith and repentance.

When we come to the Lord's Table for Holy Communion, with faith and repentance, the visible Word (the body and blood of Jesus Christ) brings us the Spirit of Christ.

Imagine your life as a Baptismal Font, for that is where your life with God began. You were baptized in the name of the Father, Son, and Holy Spirit. Your Christian life began when the Holy Spirit came in you. On that day in your life, he descended. He came *in* you and filled you with himself!

And a marvelous, mysterious, transformation took place. Dr. John Ward, Jr., and his wife, Ruthie, are good friends of ours. When I came into the ministry, John Ward, Sr., (John's father) was my first District Superintendent in the Methodist Church. He used to tell of preaching a revival in the Kentucky hills. A mean, tough, rough, old mountain man responded to the Gospel message and gave his life to Christ. Then Dr. Ward told him he needed to have the new relationship sealed in the waters of Christian baptism. The man reluctantly agreed, for he was very much afraid of water, but insisted if he were to be baptized, it must be by immersion. The only place available for immersion in those Kentucky hills was the pit of an old mine quarry. It was filled with dirty, brackish, lime water and was not the best place, but it was all that was handy for the baptism. The Sunday afternoon came, the crowd gathered, and the hesitant new convert came forward to be baptized. He was having second thoughts about it and was terrified that he would drown. Besides, the water smelled to high heaven, and what seemed like a good idea a few days before had now lost a lot of its enchantment. He said to Dr. Ward, "You won't let me drown, will you?" Dr. Ward assured him he would be perfectly safe. "You really think this is necessary?" Again Dr. Ward told him it was a vital part of his new relationship with Christ. "You think all of this is going to make a new man out of me?" Dr. Ward said, "Yes, I promise you, you will be different when the Holy Spirit takes over your life!" The mountain man said, "All right, Reverend, I'll do it, but if I'm not different when this is over, I'm gonna KILL you!" And Dr. Ward reported, "You know, he *was* different! God took that wretched, mean, evil-mouthed old sinner and made him one of the finest Christians I have ever seen!"

A couple years ago, my John and I were guests in the home of Dr. and Mrs. Robert Boyd. Dr. Boyd is a professor at the Luther-Northwestern Seminary in St. Paul, where my John served as visiting professor of Homiletics for one year. Also guests for dinner that evening were missionaries to Tanzania (in Africa), Orville and June Nyblade. They told us of the Masai women (a certain tribe in that country) who are demon possessed. These women fall into fits much like epileptic seizures. When they begin their catechetical instruction, many of them improve; at their baptism, they may be in the middle of these strange, terrifying seizures to which they are subject, but when they are baptized, they immediately become calm and well, and the seizures, after baptism, never return!

Would you not say, then, that the devil is cast out by baptism? Why not? After all, we are supposed to become "new creatures in Christ Jesus." One of the questions asked in many churches at the time of baptism is, "Will you renounce the devil and all his works and ways?" Baptism truly is a divine exorcism!

Once in awhile we find someone who says, "But I want to be re-baptized!" "I think I understand it better now," or "I'm going to the Holy Land, and I want to be re-baptized in the River Jordan, where Jesus was baptized!" Friend, we do *not* believe in re-baptism!

That is to negate the work of God that was done for you at your first baptism. No matter how you "felt" about it, God did *his* part, and you were received by his wondrous mercy and grace and became his own dear child at your first baptism!

There Is Not a Second Baptism!

Some believe they have been, at a later time, baptized in the Holy Spirit, thus separating that experience from their baptism in water. It is wrong to think we only get a "little" of the Holy Spirit at conversion and a "lot" when we have a second experience. The Holy Spirit is God and God cannot be segmented. Water Baptism and Spirit Baptism do not form two separate stages in the Christian's development. They are interrelated.

Except for John's Gospel, more emphasis is placed on the Spirit in Luke than in the other Gospels. There are seventeen references to the Spirit in Luke (compared to twelve in Matthew and six in Mark), and now here, in the Book of Acts, and in our text, Luke gives us great detail as to how the Spirit works.

In Acts 19:2, the question was asked, "Did you receive the Holy Spirit when you believed?" Those people betrayed their ignorance by saying, "No, we have never even heard that there *is* a Holy Spirit." That's right where a lot of people are, ignorant of when the Spirit's reception occurs.

In this text for today, Luke is relating Peter's sermon on the Day of Pentecost, and this is the high point of the message in this second chapter of Acts. The hearers of the sermon were invited to repentance, faith, baptism, forgiveness, and the receiving of the Holy Spirit: "Repent, and let every one of you be baptized in the name of Jesus Christ for the remission of sins; and you shall receive the gift of the Holy Spirit."

It is obvious that Luke regarded water baptism in the name of Jesus Christ as the time when the baptism of the Spirit occurred. If this were not true, then to be baptized in the name of Jesus Christ and not have received the Spirit would be to say that Christ did not have the Holy Spirit either!

It is true that there are some passages in this same book of Acts which seem to say something different. In Acts 8:12-17, the Samaritans received the Holy Spirit AFTER baptism in water. In Acts 10:44, Cornelius received the Holy Spirit BEFORE he was baptized in water. This irregularity is not a contradiction, but is simply the teaching of Luke for the Jerusalem authorities (whom Peter and John represented — Acts 8:16), so they would know that even the Samaritans (whom they despised), could also receive the Holy Spirit. The deviation from the common experience by the Spirit's descent upon Cornelius and his household before baptism indicates that Peter had no choice but to baptize them. (Acts 11:17) But both of these occasions pre-suppose that it was clearly understood that the unity of water and spirit was the norm, as our text indicates.

Jesus' Great Commission in Matthew (28:19) was to further substantiate this truth that the Holy Spirit comes when we are baptized in water. Jesus said, "Go therefore and make disciples of all the nations, baptizing them in the name of the Father and of the son and of the HOLY SPIRIT."

The understanding of the Holy Spirit's work in this action is often like that of the little girl whose family lived across the street from the cemetery. Often she listened to the minister as he spoke the words of the committal service. She decided to have one of her own in her backyard. She thought she would bury her teddy bear. After digging a grave, she solemnly lowered the toy bear into the ground, saying ever so seriously the words she thought she had heard the preachers say again and again in the burial service: "In the name of the Father and of the Son and in the hole you goes!"

We cannot afford to disown the Spirit's work when we are baptized in water. Recall, too, that Paul said, " . . . one Lord, one faith, ONE baptism." (Ephesians 4:5)

But the argument persists, by those who say, "But when I received the Baptism of the Holy Spirit, it was a special, dramatic, spectacular, and life-changing event!" I don't doubt it at all. It may well have been a renewal of the Holy Spirit in the believer's life, at a time when maturity made him/her ready to receive a deeper relationship. Conversion and baptism are a once-in-a-lifetime experience, but the Holy Spirit graciously comes to us again and again and again. He may come with the gift of tongues or prophecy or healing or wisdom or another of his many gifts. We need constantly to be re-confirmed, re-anointed, re-empowered, re-newed, re-kindled, re-filled, re-assured. Hopefully, this act of the Holy Spirit comes to us repeatedly in our lives, many times over.

We may be certain that the Spirit comes always in the Sacraments of Baptism and Holy Communion, in the reading of the Word in private devotions, and as the Word is read, taught, and preached in worship, and in special ways, often unsought and unexpected. He surprises us with his presence and overwhelms us with his blessing and power!

Many Refreshing Experiences

No, there are NOT two baptisms, but there ARE many refreshing experiences. Some years ago I was invited to go to Chile with a team of other ministers on an evangelistic crusade. But, before I could go, I found that even though I had been inoculated for smallpox many years before, they still would not let me go without a booster shot. That's what we all need. Perhaps each of us should ask God for a "booster shot" of the Holy Spirit. We could begin by praying the words of the hymn:

"Breathe on me, Breath of God
Fill me with life anew;
That I may love what Thou dost love,
And do what Thou wouldst do."

13

Christians Die Well

Fourth Sunday of Easter
Acts 6:1-9, 7:2a, 51-60

Now in those days, when the number of the disciples was
multiplying, there arose a murmuring against the Hebrews by the
Hellenists, because their widows were neglected in the daily
distribution. Then the twelve summoned the multitude of the
disciples and said, "It is not desirable that we should leave the
word of God, and serve tables. Therefore, brethren, seek out from
among you seven men of good reputation, full of the Holy Spirit
and wisdom, whom we may appoint over this business; but we
will give ourselves continually to prayer and to the ministry of the
word." And the saying pleased the whole multitude. And they
chose Stephen, a man full of faith and the Holy Spirit, and Philip,
Prochorus, Nicanor, Timon, Parmenas, and Nicolas, a proselyte
from Antioch, whom they set before the apostles; and when they
had prayed, they laid hands on them. And the word of God
spread, and the number of the disciples multiplied greatly
in Jerusalem, and a great many of the priests were obedient to the
faith. And Stephen, full of faith and power, did great wonders and
signs among the people. Then there arose some from what is
called the Synagogue of the Freedmen (Cyrenians, Alexandrians,
and those from Cilicia and Asia), disputing with Stephen.

"You stiffnecked and uncircumcised in heart and ears! You
always resist the Holy Spirit; as your fathers did, so do you. Which
of the prophets did your fathers not persecute? And they killed
those who foretold the coming of the Just One, of whom you now
have become the betrayers and murderers, who have received the
law by the direction of angels and have not kept it." When they
heard these things they were cut to the heart, and they gnashed at
him with their teeth. But he, being full of the Holy Spirit, gazed
into heaven and saw the glory of God, and Jesus standing at the
right hand of God, and said, "Look! I see the heavens opened and
the Son of Man standing at the right hand of God!"

During World War II, the greatest Norwegian Lutheran churchman of the time, Bishop Elvind Berggrav, was kept prisoner under heavy Nazi guard. However, his witness was so great and his deeds and words of love so compelling, that his eleven-man guard was constantly changed to keep them from coming under his strong, spiritual influence. The Nazis knew they were dealing with a man who knew Christ, and they dared not take any chances with him. How he loved his enemies!

This is the kind of man who is our example in today's text. Stephen was one of seven deacons chosen to "serve tables" in the First Church of Jerusalem. This was not a job as a waiter in a restaurant. It was a job which was created to help the Apostles with administrative problems so they could give full time to preaching the gospel.

There were two kinds of Jews in Jerusalem who had converted to the Christian faith: Hellenist Jews and Palestinian Jews. The Hellenists were Jews who spoke Greek and who had come from foreign countries, made the discovery of Christ, and had stayed in Jerusalem. The Palestinian Jews spoke Aramaic and Hebrew, were rigidly orthodox, and looked with contempt upon the "foreign" Jews. The Hellenistic widows felt they were being neglected in the daily distribution to the needy. So seven deacons, all Hellenist Jews, were elected to oversee the apportionment of the monies and provisions for the needy in the fellowship. One of the seven, a man named Stephen, was the head of the list of new deacons, and without him the whole course of the history of the Christian Church might have been different.

Stephen Was a Man
"Full of Faith and the Holy Spirit" (verse 5)

The Holy Spirit brings us to faith, and faith brings us to new life in Christ. Of all the things to admire in Stephen, probably his faith stands first. He had given himself so completely and unreservedly to Christ, that at no time do we see him doubting that the living, resurrected Lord was with him. Oh, for a faith like that — a faith that does not faint in any battle and refuses to despair in any situation! William H. Bathhurst, in the nineteenth century, wrote the same prayer in his hymn:

"O for a faith that will not shrink,
Tho' pressed by every foe,
That will not tremble on the brink
Of any earthly woe!"

Stephen's faith was in the essentials. He was filled with the Holy Spirit, and his faith in Jesus was founded on bed-rock certainty. The rather ridiculous story is told of three men of God who were once walking together in the forest, and the conversation turned to the nature of faith. They disagreed on what it is, what it can do, and who among them had the strongest faith. The first man pointed to a tree ahead which was leaning ever so slightly with the wind. He said, "I have the faith that God can send a wind and blow that tree down now." And the tree fell down! It was a marvelous feat, and he surprised even himself. The second man said, "You picked a tree that was already leaning. I'll pick one that is strong and straight, and I'll pray God that the wind will come and blow it down." He prayed long and hard, and a terrible wind came from the north, and of all the trees in the forest, it was only the one he selected that fell to the ground. He could hardly believe his own faith. The third man picked a tree, straight and strong and powerful, and said, "Faith alone is powerful, and needs no wind. I command this tree to fall without the wind." And that tree fell with a mighty thud. The three men were terribly pleased with themselves until they heard a deep, booming voice in the woods, "Who's tearing up my forest? If you must exercise your faith, do it where it matters!" Stephen's faith was exerted, not in silly things, but in Christ who had given him forgiveness and life.

Stephen's faith gave him a wonderful expectancy. It is said that people came to Charles Spurgeon's revivals and were converted, but they CAME to be converted. His faith was contagious; the fact that he EXPECTED them to be converted led people to expect it themselves. He expected it because he loved the people, because he believed they needed salvation, and because he believed in the power of the Gospel. Stephen genuinely believed that the Gospel is the power of God and that faith in Christ could and would change people from walking in darkness to light.

Stephen witnessed unashamedly to his faith. I have recently read a book about revival by a Baptist preacher in Texas, whose name is John Bisagno. It is said that he is so happy about being a child of God that he will strike up conversations with anyone, anywhere. Recently he was on a plane and turned to the passenger sitting next to him, saying, "How do you like the airline?" The passenger replied, "Pretty well." Then John responded, "Thank you. Thank you very much. My father owns the airline!" Then he hummed a bit and said casually, "He owns A T & T, too." Then he added, "He also owns Westinghouse and DuPont and General Motors." By this time he had the full attention of the passenger, who asked, "Who *is* your father, anyway?" Then Bisagno replied, "I thought you'd never ask!" Then he shared his faith in his Father, the God who owns the world.

Stephen Was a Man "Full of Grace and Power" (verse 8)

Because of his faith in Christ who had saved him through his unlimited, unending, unfathomable love, Stephen was a radically different person. Graciousness became a part of every fiber of him. Faith in Christ had redeemed him, grace had aided his maturity, and the power of the Holy Spirit accompanied his words and actions. When Golda Meir of Israel met the President of the United States, the President said to her, "I want one of your generals, Moishe Dayan." Meir replied, "I want *two* of your generals, General Electric and General Motors." Certainly these corporations are powerful, but there is something far more powerful and influential. It is the Gospel, and it had harnessed Stephen with its power and made him a dynamo for God!

The nuclear arms race has made us conscious of military power. *Christian Century* (May 4, 1983) reported this year that the U.S. has enough warheads to destroy all 218 Soviet cities with 100,000 or more population, at least forty times over. But Stephen's power makes that power look puny, for his power was an "inner security force" that had convinced him that *God* was his refuge and strength in every time of trouble.

Stephen Had the Gift of "Wisdom" (verse 3)

The Holy Spirit which gave Stephen power also gave him wisdom. It was a God-inspired insight, sensitivity, discernment, and understanding that directed his life. He could see the long view of things, as God sees them.

His reasoning and logic were not as shortsighted as the man who decided to manufacture dog food. He said, "I'll use all the selling arts. I'll design an alluring can, an eye-arresting label, catchy slogans, and jingles. I'll blanket the media with advertising. I'll use coupons. I'll use direct mail, and I'll have conspicuous displays in all the big stores." He did all these things, but the dog food barely sold at all. So he went to a pet store and asked, "Why doesn't my dog food sell?" The store manager answered, "Because the dogs don't *like* it!" Sometimes the wisdom of God is just good, common sense, and Stephen knew it.

We've been talking about Stephen in the glowing terms that Luke used to describe him. Let us look at some of the events that led up to his death:

Stephen's Story

Being a Christian with faith, grace, power, wisdom, and the Holy Spirit doesn't mean you will have no problems . . . and Stephen had plenty!

Stephen became far more than an able administrator of gifts for the widows and needy. Signs and wonders followed his work among the people. And then he went to a Synagogue service and began to teach and preach that the Jesus of Nazareth whom they had crucified was the Messiah! No one could withstand him — his words and spirit were irresistible. So, when the Jews found their logic and argument failed them in the force of his wisdom, their last recourse was force, so they arrested Stephen.

He was brought before the Sanhedrin, and there he gave his sermon, which is the longest address in the Book of Acts. His face shown like an angel as he proclaimed that Christ would give them a fresh, new, exciting relationship with God. It would supersede the old law and the bondage of their present religion.

Boldly, Stephen declared that the religious leaders were "stiffnecked people, uncircumcised in heart and ears, who would always resist the Holy Spirit." Not only did he tell them their faults, but he proclaimed that Jesus was the Messiah of the Jews, he was also the Son of God, and the final insult to them was that he declared that Jesus was the Son of man. To the Jews, that meant Jesus was the Savior of the World — the WORLD, not just the Jews! They couldn't tolerate that! That would mean they were no longer "special," "favored," the "elect," the "privileged," the "exclusive." ALL the nations could now be saved. This news ignited their wrath and fury to violence and they stoned Stephen to death, thus making him the first Christian martyr, or "witness," to die for the faith. They took him to a high place and pushed him off into a pit. That didn't kill him, so they hurled huge stones and boulders down on him until he finally died.

He lived with faith, wisdom, and power. And never forget that HOW WE LIVE DETERMINES HOW WE DIE!

Stephen Died Forgiving His Enemies (verse 60)

Stephen learned the spirit of forgiveness from Jesus, the One he loved and served. Look how similar their death-prayers are as they prayed for those who killed them. Jesus said, "Father, forgive them for they know not what they do." Stephen said, "Lord, do not charge them with this sin." Christians do not hold grudges against those who injure, hurt, or even kill them. We never pray better than when we pray the prayer our Lord taught us: "Forgive us our trespasses, as we forgive those who trespass against us."

Forgiveness is a lesson and spirit which comes slowly to some of us. A friend tells about two children who often argued before bedtime. One evening, following a particularly bad fight, the brother and sister were still angry with each other when they went to bed. After midnight, an earth-shattering storm awakened the members of the family. The parents heard an unusual noise down the hall near the children's bedrooms. Listening carefully, the father heard the children in the closet. "What are you doing in there?" he called out. A small, terrified voice answered, "We're in the closet forgiving each other."

Forgiveness must be genuine if God is to forgive us in return. A Scottish story tells of a man who feared he was on his deathbed. He sent for an acquaintance with whom he had had a bitter feud many years before. They had been enemies all that time. Now the dying man made an overture of peace. Finally, they settled the old quarrel, shook hands, and the other man prepared to leave the room. As he walked out the door of the sick room, the dying man feebly and weakly roused himself on one elbow and said, "But remember, if I get well, our old quarrel still stands!" Stephen's forgiveness of his enemies was more honest than that. With his dying breath, he prayed for those who caused his death.

Stephen Died Without Fear (verse 60)

As the stones hailed down upon his body; bruised, bleeding, and broken, Stephen prayed for his enemies and died. But note how the Scripture describes his death, "And when he said this, he fell asleep."

"Fell asleep" — can you imagine anything more calm and tranquil and peaceful than that? Killed by horrible violence, but the reaction of this Christian is peace. He simply went to sleep. This comforting terminology should help to assuage our fears as we contemplate our own death. Jesus said of the twelve-year-old girl whom he restored to life, "The child is not dead, but sleeping." (Mark 5:39) Paul said to the Corinthian Christians, "We shall not all *sleep* (die), but we shall all be changed . . ." (1 Corinthians 15:51) Now that's not scary, is it? The Christian can face death with confidence, trust, fearlessness, calm, and perfect peace.

Because it is facing the unknown, many people are afraid of death. A minister came to me recently and requested prayer because he was literally terrified when he thought about his own death. I know another pastor who is very insecure when he visits the sick in hospitals or is asked to conduct a funeral, because he cannot face the subject of death. This fear can haunt and intimidate us all of our living days, or we can put an end to it by our total confidence and trust in God.

An old Indian fable tells about a mouse that lived in mortal fear of cats. So the old medicine man turned the mouse into a cat, but immediately it became fearful of dogs. The medicine man then turned him into a dog, but then he was afraid of wolves. Then the medicine man turned him into a wolf, and then he was fearful of hunters. Finally, the wise Indian told him, "I can do nothing for you because you have the heart and the mentality of a mouse!" So he turned him back into a mouse. The spirit of fear can become a way of life for us. It will rule us like a cruel despot and keep us from realizing all the joy God intended us to have in the days of our lives. Paul wrote to Timothy, "For God hath not given us the spirit of *fear,* but of power and of love and of a sound mind." (2 Timothy 1:7)

I recently read, on the same day, from two different sources, the experiences of two cancer victims as they faced death. The non-Christian said, "I have come out of nowhere and am going back into it whence I came. My consciousness will come to an end. The big eye of the brain will close up shop and go out of business.

The magic of living will be over. I was a being and meant something. Soon I will be no different from a grain of sand." Isn't that a fatalistic outlook? Isn't that heart-breakingly sad? Isn't there a pitiful poignancy about the expression of no hope, no future, no life?

Consider the other dying person, who said, "I learned that I had cancer. God used my circumstances to teach me many things and to draw me closer to him than I have ever been. God did not cause the cancer, but he came to me in that situation and poured out blessings upon me that I might never have received otherwise. I realize that, as a Christian, I have nothing to fear, not even my own death. What a blessing to find the strength promised in the Bible is a reality to me now!" A hymn often sung at a Christian funeral says,

"Asleep in Jesus! blessed sleep!
From which none ever wake to weep;
A calm and undisturbed repose,
Unbroken by the last of foes.

Asleep in Jesus! Oh, how sweet
To be for such a slumber meet!
With holy confidence to sing
That death has lost its venomed sting!"

Christians Die Well

You and I may never be martyred, as was Stephen, for the cause of Christ. Our death may come, not by stoning, but by cancer, heart attack, violence, accident, or some other unknown. But if we *live* like Stephen, full of faith and the Holy Spirit, we can also *die* like him, forgiving all wrongs done to us and in fearless confidence simply "fall asleep."

John Wesley came home from preaching one day

and, seeing his brother Charles feeling low and much discouraged about the work, said, "Keep on preaching. Don't give up! OUR PEOPLE DIE WELL!"

14
Which Jesus? — This Jesus!

Fifth Sunday of Easter
Acts 17:1-15

" . . . This Jesus whom I preach to you is the Christ."

A conductor said to the Lt. Governor of the State of Pennsylvania, as he was boarding a train, "Go right up the steps, sir, turn left, and take a seat." But the Lt. Governor turned right instead of left and found himself in an empty car. He had just settled himself down when some twenty people, all dressed exactly alike, came in the car. The conductor said, "Sir, I think you'll want to move into the other car. You see, these people are all from the mental hospital." "No, I'll just stay right here," the Lt. Governor responded. Pretty soon a guard came in and began counting his patients, saying, "One, two, three, three, four, five . . ." and coming to the man who was dressed differently from the rest, he asked, "Who are you?" He answered, I'm the Lt. Governor of the State of Pennsylvania." "Oh," said the guard, "six, seven, eight, nine . . ."

It is only a made-up story, of course, but it makes the point that dealing with identity is always a pertinent issue. This is the case before us in the text. Who *was* Jesus? *Which* Jesus was he? But first, let's remember the background of the story that raises the question.

Last Sunday we read and heard of Stephen, the first Christian martyr, who was stoned to death for the Christian faith. But while he was dying and praying for his enemies, a young, brilliant, intellectual named Saul of Tarsus stood by, consenting to his death. He may even have held the garments of those who flung stones at Stephen and killed him. Saul saw Stephen's bloody, forgiving, shining-like-an-angel-face and was never the same again!

Augustine said, "If St. Stephen had not spoken thus, if he had not prayed thus, the Church would not have had Paul." The Jesus that Stephen died for captured the attention of Saul of Tarsus on a Damascus Road, claimed him for his own and thus (in my opinion), the greatest Christian of all times was born: the Apostle Paul.

Paul preached the gospel in Philippi and many were brought to faith in Christ. Now, in today's lesson, Paul is in the city of Thessalonica, in the Synagogue, preaching again. It is a vital place for this prince of missionaries to herald the Gospel. Thessalonica is located on the famous Roman Road, named the Egnatian Way, that led from the Adriatic Sea to the Middle East. The central avenue of Thessalonica was part of that road, so if the Christian faith is firmly planted in Thessalonica, it will traverse from east to west. Paul, for three Sabbaths, reasoned, explained, and demonstrated the Scriptures to his hearers in the Synagogue. His message of Jesus was the same as it would be to the Corinthians and wherever else he traveled, "For I determined not to know anything among you except Jesus Christ and Him crucified." (1 Corinthians 2:2)

He told the Thessalonicans that "Christ had to suffer and rise again from the dead." Then, to make certain he was not misunderstood, he continued, "This Jesus whom I preach to you is the Christ."

Notice his emphasis on "this Jesus!" The name was a common one in Jesus' and Paul's day. It was derived from "Joshua." Paul pointed to *one certain person* by the name of Jesus, not just *any* Jesus who happened to be walking around town. It was "this Jesus" who suffered and died on a cross, it was "this Jesus" who rose from the dead. Paul unashamedly and boldly made the claim that "this Jesus" is the Christ. He is Savior, Messiah, Deliverer, God's only Son, who came to reconcile the world to God.

The result of Paul's proclamation was that "some of them were persuaded" (Acts 17:4) and some "were not persuaded." (Acts 17:5)

It is not so different today, is it? Some believe in "this Jesus" of the Scriptures, and some are still "not persuaded."

It is imperative that we examine "which Jesus" it is in whom we place our trust. "Which Jesus?" — "This Jesus!"

"This Jesus" Is the Greatest Teacher

We owe much to great teachers of the past. Who of us has not had a good teacher that he/she does not still recall with a debt of gratitude? I'm sure many come to mind just now, as they do to me, but I think I shall never forget my first-grade teacher. Her name was Vera Busick, and I cannot call her face to mind. I thought she was beautiful, but that may have been because I still remember her sweetness, patience, and kindness to me. It was she who instilled in me a love for words and reading. She found how easily I was addicted to books, so she let me expand as much as my capacities allowed. The old-time spelling-bees were a part of our one-room school excitement, and I always will remember the heady triumph of "winning" over the FIFTH graders. For that victory she gave me a book (naturally) as a prize. It was the first book I ever owned, and I literally wore it out reading it. How wise she was.

Not all teachers and speakers are so wise. Economist John Kenneth Galbraith relayed, with keen good humor, his wife's comment on the lengthiness of his speeches. "She says," he reported to an audience, "that people may not be a great deal wiser after my talks, but they are always a great deal older!"

Great minds have always fascinated us and put us in their debt. Civilization will forever be indebted to the great minds of Greece, Palestine, and Rome. Rome taught men to rule. The Phoenician was the greatest of the early navigators and the inventor of the European alphabet. Greece taught men to think. The Jew was the schoolmaster in religion. Who could discount the value of minds like Socrates, Plato, Aristotle, and Jesus?

Who would ever presume to question that Jesus was not a great teacher? Even the agnostic or the atheist could accept that the teachings of Jesus come from a great heart, a great spirit, and a great mind. He taught that we should "love one another." Who could deny the merit in that? He taught that "Whatsoever you want others to do to you, do also to them." (Matthew 7:12) The world readily accepts this axiom and names it "The Golden Rule."

As a young man, just twelve years of age, Jesus was found in the temple, listening to the teachers and asking questions. And those men, some of them the finest thinkers of their time, were astonished at his understanding and answers.

He taught "as one having authority." More than any other sage, he taught us of God. Those who heard his beatitudes, his parables, his words of wisdom and power, finally had to say, "Never man spake like this man."

You can think of Christ as an ancient teacher, and he was. But he is likewise of today and tomorrow. His Spirit, his words, his teachings, are as modern as the six o'clock news. His teachings belonged to his time, but not more than to ours. Jesus' teachings are at home in all centuries. Hear him, and you cry, "I have listened to the world's greatest Teacher!"

This I say about "this Jesus," but there is more, much more . . .

"This Jesus" Is the Only Savior

Jesus, "this Jesus," will forever be linked with a cross and an empty tomb. Nowhere in his letters does Paul ever speak of the death of Christ without also mentioning his resurrection. Christ's death and resurrection are two sides of the same invaluable coin.

"This Jesus" has redeemed some pretty rough people by his death and life: a thief on a cross, a tax-collector named Zacchaeus, a seven-demon-possessed woman named Mary Magdalene, murderers, thieves, drug addicts, alcoholics, liars, adulterers, prostitutes, people-in-love-with-only-themselves, and even YOU and ME!

When we see the cross of "this Jesus," we know we have beheld the world's greatest love. Paul knew this Christ was not for hiding but for revelation. He knew if we could see "this Jesus," then Christianity would forever be visible to us.

A good, hard, long, contemplative look at "this Jesus" of cross and resurrection brings heavy conviction upon us. You don't hear that phrase often anymore. We used to talk about "conviction," meaning conviction of sin. It is a moral defeat when we don't know we are sinners. You can't persuade, bully, or argue another into "conviction" of his/her sinfulness. As long as we can brazenly assert, "I am not as bad as others," "I haven't done anything wrong," "After all, I'm only human," as long as we can gloat on ourselves with great self-satisfaction, there is not much hope for us. There can be no colossal goodness in life without first having a consciousness of sin. I like to pray daily, because I need it so much, "Lord, be merciful to me a sinner." We *are* sinners, we are lost, we are helpless to help ourselves, and Christ's death and life offer a way out of our insoluble problem of sin.

"This Jesus" wrote the story of redemption on a rugged cross on a hill far away. "This Jesus" invites and beseeches us to serve him. I am fully persuaded, absolutely convinced, beyond any shadow of doubt that "this Jesus" is the only Savior of the world!

"This Jesus" is the world's greatest Teacher, the world's only Savior, and more . . .

"This Jesus" Is With Us Personally

As Jesus himself drew near to the hurting disciples who walked the Emmaus Road, so he does the same for us. That's what my heart begs for, doesn't yours? — a God not afar off, but a God close by. We sing all sorts of hymns that indicate the crying need of the soul: "Just a Closer Walk With Thee," "Draw Me Nearer," "O Love That Wilt Not Let Me Go," "Still, Still With Thee," "What a Friend We Have in Jesus." Persons of all time have echoed the urgency to have a Jesus who comes in a personal, living, vital relationship with them.

When "This Jesus" Is With Us, It Means No More Fear

Fear makes us miserable; fear makes us over-react. Did you hear the story about the man who found himself in the middle of a pasture, and suddenly an angry bull came charging at him? The only escape in sight was a tree, but the nearest limb was ten feet off the ground. Because he had no choice, the man ran for the tree, made a tremendous leap, and missed! Well, he missed it on the way up, but caught it on the way down!

The story is told of a child who said to her mother, "Mama, I love you better than I love God." The mother said, "But, honey, you mustn't say that. Why would you ever say a thing like that?" But the little girl stubbornly responded, "But I do! I love you better than God." The mother said, "Well, surely you have a reason." And the child replied, "Because I can hug you, mama, and I can't hug God." The child's theology was of the heart. That is why Christ came to earth; that's what the Incarnation is all about. "This Jesus" is God manifest in the flesh, so that the world could "hug" him. Jesus draws near to us, and his presence takes away all fear. A recent newspaper article said that everyone needs at least eight hugs a day! I'm sure a lot of people do not get them, but Jesus is nearer to us than hands and feet and breathing, and his nearness encompasses us in the "Hug of Heaven!"

When "This Jesus" Is With Us, It Means Rest

Everybody gets tired. We live such hectic, busy, frenetic lives. Demands are made upon us mentally, physically, and emotionally. Spouses make demands on each other, our work insists we keep going no matter how tired we are, and children make unending and unbelievable claims upon our energies. Did you hear of the four couples who decided to rent a summer house for two months? Each couple would take a two-week vacation at the summer house, and take the thirteen children of the four families with them for two weeks. One woman was bragging to a friend how clever the plan was when the friend said, "I can't imagine that two weeks in a cabin with thirteen kids could ever be called a vacation." Her friend said — "Absolutely not! Those two weeks are bad beyond description, but the vacation is the six weeks at home *without* the children!"

Jesus said, "Come unto Me, and I will give you rest." Horatius Bonar wrote reassuring words in his hymn which says,

> "I heard the voice of Jesus say, 'Come unto Me
>   and rest;
> Lay down, thou weary one, lay down thy head
>   upon My breast.'
> I came to Jesus as I was, Weary, worn and sad;
> I found in Him a resting place, and He has
>   made me glad."

For the tired, fatigued, nervous, exhausted; Christ offers rest — rest for the weary.

My mother had ten children and labored long and hard hours to keep them fed, clean, and properly clothed. She washed the clothes for us, most of her life, on a wash board. Laundry day was every Monday, and she washed the clothes by hand, scrubbing on the wash board until her knuckles would bleed where she had literally worn the skin off of them. She ironed for us all with an old flat iron. She cooked meals on a wood stove in the winter and on a cantakerous old kerosene stove in the summer. She kept the house spotlessly neat and clean. She loved Jesus with a pure heart and sang the great hymns of the church around the house, all day long, as she worked. But she often would admit, "My feet hurt." Why wouldn't they hurt? The shoes she wore were sometimes too small because they had been given to her by someone else. Often they were worn through on the soles, or run-over on the sides. As a result of wearing ill-fitting shoes and standing long hours on her feet, my mother developed corns and bunions and sore feet. We didn't have a car, so we walked everywhere we went, even to church. And mother never missed church! She was there for Sunday School and church every Sunday morning. She walked back every Sunday evening for the service. She attended every Wednesday night prayer meeting. When a revival was in progress, mother attended every service, even if it lasted for two or three weeks. Sometimes, when we would see how tired she was, how her feet hurt her, we'd ask her not to go to church that night: "Why not just stay home and rest?" we'd ask. Her reply was always the same, "Why, child, it RESTS me to go to church. I always feel so much better by the time the service is over." The personal presence of "this Jesus" literally invigorated her.

What would it do for the ulcer-causing, nerve-frazzling exhaustion of our time if we could learn to "rest" in "this Jesus"?

"This Jesus" Is All the Good Things You Know Personally

"This Jesus " is all the good you can know about: peace, hope, love, pardon, understanding, faith, and kindness. I read of a little, old, grey-haired man who stood over the bedside of his dying wife. She seemed to be trying to tell him something, so he tenderly bent beside her bed, bending near to hear her response to his question: "What do you want, dear? What do you want?" And her feeble answer was, "I want you. I want you."

"This Jesus" — this PERSONAL Jesus — draws near and says to our hearts, in the very hour you read this, "What do you want, dear? What do you want?" If our hearts have any vision at all, they will answer, "I want you, Jesus. I want you!" And he himself will draw

122

near and won't go away forever, for he says, "I am with you always, even unto the end of the world."

A lovely story is told of a king who asked his three daughters how much they loved him. Two of them replied that they loved him more than all the gold and silver in the world. The third, the youngest, said, "I love you better than salt." The king was not especially elated with her answer and lightly dismissed it as an indication of her immaturity. But the cook overheard the conversation and the next morning left the salt out of everything in the king's breakfast. Then, pushing his plate aside, he realized the deep meaning of his daughter's remark. In saying, "I love you more than salt," she was in reality saying, "I love you so much that nothing is any good without you." Isn't that the bottom line of our experience as related to Christ? "Nothing is any good in life unless we have 'This Jesus!'"

"This Jesus!"

You have surely suspected (if you've read this book thus far, or any of my other books) that there are literally hundreds of Gospel songs and hymns that speak deeply to my soul, and if you would ask, "Barbara, 'Which Christ' is yours?" I'd have no trouble at all responding, "*This* Christ." Part of the depth of my feeling is expressed in the words of this Gospel song:

"All my life was full of sin when Jesus found me,
All my heart was full of misery and woe;
Jesus placed His strong and loving arms around me,
And He led me in the way I ought to go.

No one ever cared for me like Jesus,

There's no other Friend so kind as He;
No one else can take the sin and darkness from
    me —
O how much He cares for me!"

In Shakespeare's *King Lear,* when the king was dying, with faltering lips he muttered, "Cordelia." The dying lips of Napoleon whispered, "Head of the Army." But if we know Christ as Savior and personal Friend, when our lips stammer, when sight grows dim, when hands grow still, when we can hear human voices no more, we can whisper, not "Cordelia," not "Head of the Army," but "Jesus, Jesus, 'This Jesus!' "

15
"Sneak Up On 'Em!"

Sixth Sunday of Easter
Acts 17:22-34

Then Paul stood in the midst of the Areopagus and said, "Men of Athens, I perceive that in all things you are very religious; for as I was passing through and considering the objects of your worship, I even found an altar with this inscription:
TO THE UNKNOWN GOD.
Therefore the One whom you worship without knowing, Him I proclaim to you: God who made the world and everything in it, since He is Lord of heaven and earth, does not dwell in temples made with hands. Nor is He worshiped with men's hands, as though He needed anything, since He gives to all life, breath, and all things. And He has made from one blood every nation of men to dwell on all the face of the earth, and has determined their preappointed times and the boundaries of their habitation, so that they should seek the Lord, in the hope that they might grope for Him and find Him, though He is not far from each one of us; for in Him we live and move and have our being, as also some of your own poets have said, 'For we are also His offspring.' Therefore, since we are the offspring of God, we ought not to think that the Divine Nature is like gold or silver or stone, something shaped by art and man's devising. Truly, these times of ignorance God overlooked, but now commands all men everywhere to repent, because He has appointed a day on which He will judge the world in righteousness by the Man whom He has ordained. He has given assurance of this to all, by raising Him from the dead."
And when they heard of the resurrection of the dead, some mocked, while others said, "We will hear you again on this matter." So Paul departed from them. However, some men joined him and believed, among them Dionysius the Areopagite, a woman named Damaris, and others with them.

George Whitefield once said,

"I'm willing to go to prison for you,
I'm willing to go to death with you,
But I'm not willing to go to heaven
    without you!"

Not everyone likes or agrees with the Apostle Paul,
but few discount his magnificent mind and his passion
to make Christ known. He was a man for all seasons
and cleverly planned his strategy for the most
effectiveness.

This master communicator, guided by the Holy
Spirit, had preached in Philippi, Thessalonica, Beroea,
and now, before he goes on to Corinth, he makes a
stop in Athens. Athens was a city "full of idols," with
a whole regiment of altars to unknown gods. Paul
stopped at one of these altars and began to preach.
Let us learn some lessons in witnessing from this
superb evangelist.

Begin Where the People Are (verses 22-23)

Paul, with his unique audience in mind, begins
where they are. He takes a known to present an
unknown to them. "Men of Athens," he began, "I
perceive that in every way you are very religious. For
as I passed along, and observed the objects of your
worship, I found also an altar with this inscription, 'To
an unknown God.' What therefore you worship as
unknown, this I proclaim to you."

He began by getting their attention, and then was
off-and-running with the eloquent oratory and skill for
which he is so well-known. Paul had drunk deeply of
the well of salvation, had become addicted to the
Water of Life, and his passion for Christ had made him
a peddler of the same "spiritual high" which he had

experienced. This kind of ardor for others is not learned, nor shamed into us, nor programmed into us, nor even educated into us; it is simply impossible for one who has found Jesus as Savior and realized the riches of that "find" to be silent. We become "spiritual arsonists," intentionally and deliberately setting people on fire for God!

People are won for Christ, primarily, by someone speaking to them about Christ and the Church. Charles Wesley wrote a hymn entitled, "O for a Thousand Tongues to Sing My Great Redeemer's Praise." A thousand tongues would be fine (maybe), but we would be glad to settle for just one! If every tongue of every Christian would be dedicated, sanctified, and consecrated to tell the Gospel story, we would soon set the world aflame!

There are multitudes of ways for evangelism to take place. Methods are as varied as are the witnesses; some are naturally better than others. Someone found fault with D.L Moody's methods of evangelism. He responded, "I like my way of doing it better than your way of *not* doing it!" The worst we can do is to do nothing at all.

Paul was very wise in his approach. If you are going to catch fish, deer, quail, or people, it is sometimes best to "Sneak up on 'em." This is certainly not to say we are going to be dishonest, manipulative, or misrepresentative at any time, but it *is* to say we are going to be aware that a lot of folks are "running-scared" of religion; they are leery of the "hard-sell" that has turned them off and are rightly suspicious of people whose motives are to "get 'em" so they can carve another notch in their Gospel Gun of converts.

Communication, at best, is not easy. Two men went into a restaurant and saw that there were three vegetables on the menu from which to choose. The waitress said to them, "Just tell me which one of the three you don't want, it will be a lot easier that way." One fellow said, "I don't want any rutabagas," but rutabagas weren't even on the menu. She said, "Look, mister, you can't not want something we haven't got, you've gotta not want something we have!"

Paul started where his hearers were. Jesus told us to be "wise as serpents and harmless as doves." We manage the "harmless as doves" part fairly well, but our "wisdom" is often astoundingly lacking.

The one who is witnessing must follow Christ closely if he/she expects to be heard. Nietzsche was not unfair when he said, "You will have to look more redeemed if I am to believe in your Redeemer." Laurence Houseman said, "A saint is one who makes goodness attractive." Do we enhance the Gospel we represent, or bring a reproach upon it?

Paul didn't begin by using a sledgehammer of verbal accusations to those he addressed. He might have said, "Shame on you, Athenians, for having so many gods," or "How can you possibly worship an 'unknown' God?" or "You claim to be philosophers and don't know who God really is! Where are your brains?!" NO! Rather, he started with them.

If those to whom we witness do not know God the Father as revealed in Christ, we do not and should not criticize or assault their intelligence. We might do well to start by talking about "their" gods. There are all kinds of gods today. Just because something seems real, doesn't mean it is. Non-Christians have a wide range of gods. It might be a rock group. It may be a media personality. It could be a star like the late Elvis Presley. He was a god to thousands who still bow before the shrine of his grave at Graceland in Memphis, Tennessee. Or consider the god of Transcendental Meditation, or the followers of Mysticism, or the Eastern religions. Some thirty-two million Americans express a belief in astrology and let a dead, burned-out star in outer space decide their destiny. Or others make gods of their children, grandchildren, money, business, wife, husband, car, house, golf game, or sex. Probably the most popular god of our time is named SELF. Why not talk about "their" gods first, not critically, not judgmentally, not with a holier-than-thou attitude, but with honest interest? Paul did exactly that. He said, "I see that you are very religious, I've considered your objects of worship."

Talk About God (verses 24-28)

Then Paul, having identified with his audience, subtly began to talk about the true God, not their god, not just any god, but GOD! Note that he is still finding common ground for agreement. Everyone needs a god. An atheist said to a man who was witnessing to him, "I don't believe in God." The man wisely said, "Tell me about the god you don't believe in. Maybe I don't believe in him either!"

Paul started at the beginning, with God as Creator, the Source of all life. He told how God guided history and is the One on Whom all life depends. We live "in Him" and "we are His offspring," meaning we don't even take a breath without his giving it to us. He found contact with the people on the grounds of our common humanity.

Then Paul proceeded to instruct that God is the center of the physical and spiritual universe. If somehow, someway, we could "sneak up on 'em" with the wondrous knowledge that all their soul's needs are met in God, we would do people so much good. The soul needs God as the earth needs the sun. Because the earth has the sun, it can grow forests and gardens and flowers; it can create rivers and seas; it can live. Without the sun, our planet would be as barren as a life without love and as blind as midnight. But our earth does not need the sun as much as our world needs God. God is all the hope our world has. He is Creator, Sustainer, Light, Health, Intelligence, Inspiration, Joy, Salvation. Take God out of the world and life is dead and hope becomes the despair of eternal darkness. Everything dies if God dies, even love, for God is love. If we lose God, we have lost it all!

Humankind can no more abandon God and live than safely abandon air. Our life is tied up in him. Paul said, "In Him we live and move and have our being!"

Paul began with God, the God-Creator, breath, life, and asserted that God's centrality is the reason for our very existence.

We need to let people know that it makes a difference whether or not they have the RIGHT God. Any old god won't do! Who really is your God? Whatever is FIRST is God. If you put your faith and hope and confidence in anything or anybody other than the one true God of the Bible, you will have NO God the Judgment Day, but you will have a Judge.

The next step, of course, was that Paul asked the Athenians to turn away from their old gods to the God who gave them life. Couldn't we be that wise, too? Let's ask people to "Try God."

Then Come Right Out and Say It! (verses 30-31)

We must finally come right out and say it! We must make truth clear. There is a community in Washington state which is located on a river, downstream from a large timber-cutting project. The logs are floated down the river to their destination, which is the saw mill below. It became the practice for the people to fish the logs out of the water, saw off the ends that had the company name printed on them, and build houses and buildings for themselves from them. The local minister heard about this practice and became very upset, and the following Sunday he preached a sermon with the title, "Thou shalt not steal." At the conclusion of the service, as the people filed out the door, they all told him what a fine sermon it was, so he knew they had missed the point. The next Sunday he preached on the subject, "Thou shalt not cut the ends off of other people's logs," and they got the point! (Of course, that preacher had to move to another church, but they got the point!)

When we rid ourselves of being embarrassed, of apology, of unnecessary theological jargon, when we dispense with irrelevant concepts, when we have made truth plain, then we must be direct in calling for a decision, a choice, a call to repentance. People are dying for a clear word from God. We must not make them wade through a veritable morass of trappings that only hide the Gospel.

There comes a time in the Christian witness when we must speak boldly and plainly of sin, of the need for confession and repentance, of Christ and his death and resurrection, and take the risk of being switched off by the participants in the dialogue.

Paul's message moved into the Incarnation and the forgiveness offered by "a Man whom He (God) has appointed." Then he just came right out and said it, "the Man God raised from the dead." *That* brought a response! To accept the resurrection demanded an act of faith on the part of his audience. A God who raised the dead was not someone just to discuss, argue over, or philosophize about; this was a God who must be confronted, and that confrontation would result in acceptance or rejection.

The Incarnation is the injection of God into the blood-stream of humanity. It is the invasion by God into the soul. The resurrection of this Incarnate One means we have to deal with him one way or another.

He cannot be ignored.

Ultimately, then, our message must call people to make definite decisions for Christ. If Martin Luther had said at the Diet of Worms, "I am inclined to think . . ." he never would have launched a Reformation. It was his positive, "Here I stand, I can do no other!" that gave him his power.

It is a stupendous claim that Christians make: "Nor is there salvation in any other, for there is no other name under heaven given among men by which we must be saved." It would be a lot easier to suggest that Christ is only one way among many to God, that he offers truth just as other leaders offer truth about God. But Paul couldn't do that, and I can't either! This is not my choice but his. I cannot put Christ on the throne of my heart as one Lord among many other gods, I can only say that I am his, that I belong, body and soul, in life and in death, not to myself, but to Jesus Christ!

Some Believed! (verse 34)

Resistance to the Gospel comes in many ways. In Philippi, they put Paul in jail. In Thessalonica, there was an uproar with political overtones. In Beroea, an angry crowd was the reason the Christians sent him on a ship to safety. Here in Athens, the resistance was of the sort with which we are all familiar — they ridiculed him. The Athenian reaction of bland toleration, of ridicule, of calling him "this babbler," is not easy to take, but it can never douse the flaming zeal of the Christian who carries a desperation for the souls of men and women to win them for Jesus Christ as Savior.

Paul was not a failure at Athens. God never allows any witness to be lost. Nothing we do for him is in vain. "But some men joined him and believed, among

them Dionysius the Areopagite and a woman named
Damaris and others with them." Eusebius, the
historian, tells us that Dionysius was one of the twelve
judges of the Areopagus, and, after becoming a
Christian, later became a bishop of the church at
Athens and died a martyr for the Christian faith.
Damaris was an aristocratic woman of Athens. The
"others" probably became strong members of the
church at Athens.

When we all stand before God in the Great Day,
will anyone point to you and say, "I am a Christian
because of him/her?" Can you imagine anything worse
than going to heaven alone?

"Lord, I would not stand alone,
When I come before Thy throne,
Let me bring at least one soul, O Lord, to Thee;
Here I give myself away,
Take me, use me, Lord, I pray,
Let me lose myself and find it, Lord, in Thee!"

16

Jesus Gives Us Tomorrow!

The Ascension
Acts1:1-11

Now when he had spoken these things, while they watched, He was taken up, and a cloud received Him out of their sight. And while they looked steadfastly toward heaven as He went up, behold, two men stood by them in white apparel, who also said, "Men of Galilee, why do you stand gazing up into heaven."

And He led them out as far as Bethany, and He lifted up His hands and blessed them. Now it came to pass, while He blessed them, that He was parted from them and carried up into heaven. (Luke 24:50-51)

The story is told of a conversation that took place many years ago on New Year's Eve on the battle line of the war zone in Korea. The temperature that night was forty-two degrees below zero. Eighteen-hundred American Marines were facing one-hundred thousand Communist troops. The situation for every man was, to say the least, precarious. At midnight a supper was served to the troops, but it was only cold beans, to be eaten out of the can as the men stood beside their tanks. The newspaper correspondents assigned to the men were standing around trying to keep warm. One of them became philosophical. He noticed a large Marine whose clothes had frozen on him as hard as a board. His beard was encrusted with mud, his hands were blue from the cold. He was eating his beans with a trench knife — cold beans at 42° below 0! The correspondent said to the Marine, "If I were God and could give you one thing you'd rather have more than anything else in the world right now, what would you ask for?" The Marine mulled it over in his mind for awhile, and finally said, "I would ask you to give me tomorrow."

It is time for Jesus to ascend back to the Father, and "tomorrow" is just what he offers his disciples. Let us catch ourselves up on the details. We owe so much to Luke for some of the specifics of Jesus' leave-taking from this planet. The picture is given partly at the end of his Gospel, and more of it at the beginning of the book of Acts, which is the sequel to Luke's Gospel.

Reading both of these accounts, we learn from where it was that the Ascension took place. "Then He led them out as far as Bethany." That means the Bethany district or area and on the brow of Olivet.

Have you ever considered what it must have been like for the resurrected, soon-to-be-ascended-and-reunited-with-His-Father Jesus to have stood there that day? Many thoughts must have gone through his mind as he prepared for his departure.

It was in this area he had known deep pain and great joy. Here he had met with cruel treachery from his foes. But here he also had known abiding, true, and loving friendships. It was in these parts he had been accepted, welcomed, and surrounded by love, but also here he had been betrayed and forsaken.

He had enjoyed the hours he had spent in the home of Mary, Martha, and Lazarus at Bethany. His heart must have saddened to recall the agony of the Garden of Gethsemane, his weakness, the bloody sweat, and the betrayal of a friend. But it was also from Bethany's district that the crowds had begun the march with "Hosannas" to Jerusalem on Palm Sunday.

Jesus must have smiled as he remembered his triumph when he called Lazarus from the dead and back to life. And not far away, on another mountain just outside the Jerusalem walls, he had died in pain, shame, and darkness. Jerusalem, Bethany, Calvary — and now Olivet. Here on Olivet he prepares to leave those he loves so dearly, those who love him so imperfectly, but still the best they can.

Jesus leaves, but before he leaves them, he gives . . .

The Promise of the Spirit (Acts 1:8)

Before Jesus leaves these eleven faithless, but learning to be faithful, men, he gives them the promise of the Holy Spirit. How like him! Knowing their loss, loneliness, and weakness when he is gone, he promises them power.

When a person cannot be present at an event, he/she sometimes says, "I'll be with you in spirit." It doesn't do much good to say it, but it does express good intentions. Jesus says the same thing, "I'll be with you by the Spirit," but when Jesus says it, it means something, for he says "Spirit" with a capital "S"!

Each disciple must have felt that day, "I cannot live without you." And Jesus says, in effect, "You won't have to!" They would, even though his physical presence was gone, still be led, guided, comforted, encouraged, and empowered. Christ was not abandoning them to a hostile world.

He was promising them the Holy Spirit which would be a living grace for the days ahead. Someone once asked Dwight L. Moody, "Have you enough grace to be burned at the stake?" "No," was his reply." "Do you wish you had?" Moody said, "No, for I don't need it. What I need now is grace to live in Milwaukee three days and hold a mission."

The disciples were being promised grace sufficient for each day and each task. They were being left, but not without comfort, hope, and help. In fact, the One who had been *with* them would now be the Spirit *in* them! And what a difference it would make in their lives.

Peter, who was such a weak and dogmatic activist, who spoke before he thought and acted before he considered, would, because of the Spirit, become a man possessed! He would be possessed of power to heal, power to raise the dead. He would be given wisdom to preach, and 3,000 souls would be added to the church in one day; his wisdom in his letters would remain the heritage of the church to this day. And this transformation happened to Peter because of the Spirit living *in* him.

Before he left, Jesus gave them . . .

A Blessing (Luke 24:50)

What seemed like the disaster of their lives to the disciples was going to turn into a blessing. Victor Hugo once exclaimed, "Why was I not exiled before?" This was a score of years after Napoleon III banished him from France. Hugo had been France's most popular literary figure when the Emperor took exception to some of his political beliefs and sent him into what everybody thought would be oblivion. In his exile, he wrote his most famous and successful novels, including *Les Miserables.* He returned to France more famous than when he left.

Jesus is about to turn their disaster into blessing. We read in Luke, " . . . and lifting up his hands he blessed them." What do you suppose he said in that blessing? Would it have been the Old Testament blessing they knew and that we also love!? "The Lord bless you and keep you. The Lord make his face shine upon you and be gracious unto you. The Lord lift up his countenance upon you and give you peace."

Do you know that a blessing is what we call a benediction? I don't mean as when someone sneezes, and the other lightly says, "God bless you." It's not the casual, leave-taking-without-any-thought-of-the-Divine that flippantly says, "Go with God!" Think of it like this: When the pastor, at the close of the worship service, lifts his arms and gives the benediction, it is not really the pastor who is blessing you, but he/she, in Christ's stead, is warming your heart one more time with his blessing. Before you go out into a cold, hard, sinful world, Jesus wraps his arms around you, leaving you with his blessing: "The love of God the Father, the grace of our Lord Jesus Christ, and the communion of the Holy Spirit be upon you, now and forever." What strength for fighting the battles of life! What comfort for our grief! What solace for our fears and hurts and pain! The blessing of God is upon us! We are going to make it after all!

And, still blessing them, Jesus parts from them. Their awed, tear-filled eyes follow him up — and up — and up — and up, until their sight of his blessed form is obscured by a cloud which hides him from view. He is out of sight. But still they strain to see him just one more time, maybe just a glimpse, but when they do not see him again, they begin to comprehend that his physical presence is no more.

Yes he is gone — but not really. His bodily form is denied them, but his presence will always be theirs, for had he of the tongue-that-spoke-only-truth not said, "Lo, I am with you always!"?

In ten day's time, he would be nearer to them than he had ever been before. The Spirit would mean they could have a closeness that physical being could

138

never allow. My John and I are blessed with a oneness of spirit in our marriage, so that no matter what words are said, there is a sense of "knowing" each other beyond all externals. Far more sensitive than our relationship is the Holy Spirit to the believer. Abiding in him, God is nearer than tongue can describe. Jesus gave them . . .

The Promise of the Second Coming (Acts 1:11)

The disciples are still standing there. Can they be hoping for a chance sight of him, even though their best judgment tells them it is impossible? And suddenly they DO see something! It is not the dear, familiar form of Jesus, but they behold two strange men, dressed in white apparel. They appear before their astounded eyes. Who were they? Who knows? Could it have been Moses and Elijah, or maybe Enoch and Daniel? Their identities are not disclosed, but they do have a question for the disciples, "Men of Galilee, why keep gazing up into heaven?"

It's not a foolish question, though we have all heard absurd queries in our time. I heard about a couple who had been going together for ten years. The fellow just kept hesitating to ask the girl to marry him. Finally, they were sitting together on one of those old-fashioned porch swings that they still have down south. It was a warm summer evening, and the girl said to him, "You know, we really ought to get married." The fellow was silent for a long time, and then he said, "I guess so; but who would have us?"

This was a good question the strangers asked the disciples, "Why stay here looking into heaven?" No answer is given by the disciples, maybe because none was needed.

The men, besides the question, also had a *message* for the disciples: "This same Jesus who was taken up from you into heaven, will so come in like manner as you saw Him go into heaven." Could anything be more definite? Jesus made it safely back to the Father in heaven, and one day he will return. So, it's "good-bye" for now, but not forever!

This is the message of Ascensiontide. Christ is in heaven, exalted at the Father's right hand. Christ promised to give his Holy Spirit to all who repent and believe, and that means we need never be without Divine Presence. Christ will one day plant his feet again upon Mount Olivet, for his ascension is the pledge of the promised Parousia.

He's coming back! He said he would! You can count on it! He gives us tomorrow!

17

"Hold Your Horses!"

Seventh Sunday of Easter
Acts 1: (1-7) 8-14

" . . . wait for the Promise of the Father."

When you were a child, did your parents ever say to you, as mine said to me, "Hold your horses!" I must have heard that phrase literally hundreds of times as I was growing up: when I wanted school to be out for the summer, when I fretted because a meal was not ready, when I wanted to do something exciting "now," when I spoke too hastily, when I demanded something be done immediately, when I couldn't stand still while mother measured a hem in a skirt — I can hear it as though it were yesterday, "Hold your horses, honey! Hold your horses!"

Jesus is preparing to leave his little band of disciples and is giving them last-minute instructions. For three-and-a-half years, he taught them by word and example; for forty days after his resurrection, he continued to teach and to nurture their faith, all in preparation for his leaving. It is nearly time for his "cloud departure," and so he gives them another very important order, "He commanded them not to depart from Jerusalem, but to *wait* for the promise of the

Father." The "promise of the Father," of course, was the coming of the Holy Spirit which would take the place of Jesus' physical presence on earth.

It should be noted that the word "wait" is not passive. It carried the meaning, "to be ready and available," "to watch," "to keep in a state of expectation." A certain little boy was pestering his parents for a watch. He kept at it for weeks. Finally, his father commanded him that he was not to mention the watch anymore. The boy reluctantly obeyed, but the family, at morning devotions, had a custom of each child's giving a Bible verse from memory. The boy chose as his verse, "What I say unto you, I say unto all, 'Watch!' " Now that is being alert and in a state of expectancy, and that is O.K.

Waiting should not be interpreted as apathetic, indifferent, lethargic, or even slow. Some people are, by nature, fast, energetic, and forceful; they are typical "A's." Others, the "B's," are slow, deliberate, and careful. A man tells of his grandmother who was a real energetic go-getter, while his grandfather was slow and deliberate. One night they were awakened by a lot of noise out in the chicken house. Grandma sprang out of bed, ran to the chicken house, and found the reason for all the commotion; a large black snake was among the hens. She couldn't find anything to kill it with, so she stomped her bare foot down on the snake's head. Of course she couldn't move then, so there she stood, waiting for Grandpa, who didn't arrive until fifteen minutes later. He was fully clothed, had every button buttoned, his coat and tie on, and even his pocket watch hanging from his vest. "Well," he said cheerfully to his enraged and frantic wife, "If'n I'da knowed you had him, I wouldn't have hurried so!" Some may find it harder to wait than others, but all of us have to work hard at times to be willing to wait.

It must seem to all of us, once in a while, that

about half a lifetime is spent just waiting. We wait for the mail to come, for the phone to ring, for results of an X-ray examination, for someone to come out of surgery, for a bus or plane or train, for the check-out line in the grocery store to move, the pot on the stove to boil, for the rain to stop, for the sun to shine, for the traffic light to change — and multitudes of other things make us wait and wait and wait!

It was a big order that Jesus gave his disciples when he told them to wait. We don't like it either — waiting.

It's Hard to Wait!

My John usually has the proverbial (and actual) patience of a saint, but there are times we nearly reach an impasse because he abhors waiting so much. I like to get places early: to church, a play, the opera, the hair-dresser, a party, a meeting. I don't even mind if we are a half-hour early, because one can always read while waiting, and I hate to be late! But my John hates to be early for *anything, because he loathes* waiting! Does that kind of stalemate sound familiar to anybody reading this? Of course, I am guilty also in that there are myriads of other ways in which I don't like to wait either.

This is a "Fast Lane," — "Hurry Up!" — "Instant Everything" — "Do It Now!" —"Make it Happen" —generation. Our way of life ill prepares us for waiting. We want instant service at the gas station, the supermarket, the drive-in restaurant, the drive-in bank, and the drive-in cleaners. In some places, we now have drive-in funeral homes which let us pay our respects while we stay in the car. "The Register of Friends Who Called" is shoved to our car window, and we sign it while viewing the corpse in the display window and listening to music by Bach in the background.

Our nation somehow equates speed with progress, giving us faster boats, cars, jets, phone service, and insurance settlements. We even dream that we can improve our school system by accelerating its programs. Young marrieds want new cars, new furniture, and new homes immediately.

Our children are as up-tight and unable to wait as we are. They can't wait till birthdays or Christmas to open their presents. They can't wait till high school to date. They can't wait to go steady, to drive the car, to have sex, to get married, or to have a baby.

"Wait" is a painful word to our impetuous natures. We can't wait for people to change or to understand us, so we divorce them or break up friendships or get rid of them; we simply don't have time to "wait" for it all to come together.

We can't wait to get over a cold, so we take orange juice, aspirin, Tylenol, Contac, and whatever the latest promise for "quick relief" is.

This same frenzy spills over into our worship. We can't wait for the entire hymn to be sung, so we delete a couple of stanzas. We can't wait for the sermon to be over, so we suggest the minister shorten the message. We can't wait for the service to end, so even while the benediction is being said, we begin replacing hymnals in racks, putting on coats, and picking up pocketbooks.

Naturally, then, we can't wait for God to answer our prayers. In fact, that's one of the hardest "waits" of all! We ask for guidance and expect it yesterday, or earlier. We pray for another person's salvation and despair if it doesn't happen "soon." We lament to God, "When will this problem be over?" "When will I be better?" "Is the answer on the way?" "God, are you sure you heard me?" We want God to work by *our* calendars, by *our* time clocks, and by *our* judgments, but if God is God, then *he's* in charge of the schedule!

Amid all of life's surging activity, we simply must take time to wait!" "They that wait upon the Lord shall renew their strength." (Isaiah 40:31)

> "Be *still,* my soul: the Lord is on thy side;
> Bear *patiently* the cross of grief or pain;
> Leave to thy God to order and provide;
> In ev'ry change He faithful will remain.
> Be still, my soul: thy best thy heav'nly Friend
> Thro' thorny ways leads to a joyful end."

In the business of life and in trusting in God, we need to learn to be still and wait. If we ever learn this good lesson, we would receive far more power and courage and peace.

Waiting Indicates Faith

If you have an appointment with someone, and if that person is late, or appears to be, your continued waiting for him/her to arrive indicates your faith in his/her word. The disciples were able to wait and wait and wait in the upper room for the Holy Spirit to come because they had learned that the word of Jesus is always good.

David was able to say, "I waited patiently for the Lord, and He heard me." Waiting is an exercise in faith, whether you wait for a human or for God.

In the waiting times, God prepares us for the next step we are to take with him. If we want to amount to something as a Christian, we must let waiting become a virtue. When James A. Garfield was head of Hiram College in Ohio, a father came into his office and asked him if the course of study couldn't be simplified so that his son might be able to "go through by a faster route." "Certainly," Garfield replied, "but it all depends upon what you want to make of your boy.

When God wants to make an oak tree, he takes a hundred years, when he wants to make a squash he requires only two months!"

When we can be fully dependent upon God, completely open, waiting, expectant, and ready to do his will, he can help us and use us in wondrous ways.

Faith is the absolute trust and confidence in God that helps us wait, no matter how slow he seems, and no matter how long our answer is in coming. The disciples waited in the upper room because Jesus said he would send the Spirit to them, and they believed him.

Waiting for Christ to help, to heal, to hear indicates that we are resting confidently in the promise of him who is utterly dependable and who said in the Word, "If we confess our sins, He is faithful and just to forgive us our sins, and to cleanse us from all unrighteousness." (1 John 1:9) No matter how we feel, no matter how unworthy, no matter what discouragement the devil whispers to our fearful hearts, we know it is so! We know God is trustworthy, and we wait!

Waiting Is Rewarded

After ten days, the Holy Spirit appeared! "And they were all filled with the Holy Spirit and began to speak with other tongues, as the Spirit gave them utterance." (Acts 2:4) Their waiting was rewarded! We never wait for God in vain! The Spirit descended and filled them *all*, just as Jesus said he would. What if they had failed to wait? What if they had given up the third day, the seventh day, the ninth day?

Legend has it that one time a man had a dream and found himself in heaven. He was taken to a huge room, containing all kinds of gifts, blessings, and marvelous things. He asked what they were, and St.

Peter replied, "Those are answers to your prayers that you simply couldn't wait for!"

There is so much in life that doesn't have to be done instantly. Day by day there are phone calls that don't have to be returned immediately. There are many difficult problems and decisions that actually improve if they are put off and left to be prayed over and to simmer in our minds awhile. Wait for prayer to be answered and you'll be surprised that it is always better, fuller, and surpassing all you had believed possible.

It's so easy to miss the point of this discipline of waiting. Bishop Armstrong tells the story of a rancher from Texas who was attending a Farmer's and Rancher's Convention in El Paso. A farmer from Rhode Island was there, and they fell into conversation. The Texan couldn't conceive of a farm in Rhode Island, so he said, "Tell me about your spread. How big is it?" The farmer from Rhode Island said, "Oh, it's about eight acres I guess." "Eight acres??!" exploded the Texan. "How can you possibly make do with just eight acres?" The farmer replied, "Well, we have chickens and sweet corn and beets and cabbage and beans. It's a good spread. How big is *your* spread?" The rancher said, "I get in my pickup in the morning and I drive west. And I drive all day. When the sun goes down, I'm still on my spread." The guy from Rhode Island said, sympathetically, "I know; I had a pickup like that once." The poor guy missed the point entirely. We have such small minds that we really can't begin to comprehend the kind of God we have who hears our prayers, answers them, and gives us far more that we asked for — but often we must wait for his right time before the answer comes.

Monica prayed for her wicked, sinful, licentious son for thirty-two years, but during all that time, do you think she ever dreamed her prayers would be heard and answered so far above and beyond her expectations? She asked for the salvation of his soul, and in his time, God gave her that, but he also made him the great Christian the world knows today as St. Augustine. If we can wait and pray on and wait and pray on and wait patiently for our answer, we will get it, and more . . . oh, so much more!

Sometimes, the reasons why we had to wait are made clear to us, but not always. Sometimes we learn that had the answer come earlier, it would have been too soon. You can't hurry God any more than you can hurry mother nature. If you force a butterfly out of its cocoon before it is time, it will die. If you rush a chick from the shell, it will die.

Joseph was in prison for two years before God freed him. Two years is a long time to be unjustly incarcerated, but his freedom worked out perfectly in the program of God, so that he could be the one who saved Egypt and his own people from starvation when the famine came.

So, "Hold your horses!" Wait with patience. God is never off schedule, never ahead of time, never behind time, but always ON time!